AF167825

Writing Skills
for University

STUDENT
SUCCESS

Writing Skills for University

From Day 1 to Dissertation

Sue Reeves

1 Oliver's Yard
55 City Road
London EC1Y 1SP

2455 Teller Road
Thousand Oaks
California 91320

Unit No 323-333, Third Floor, F-Block
International Trade Tower
Nehru Place, New Delhi – 110 019

8 Marina View Suite 43-053
Asia Square Tower 1
Singapore 018960

© Sue Reeves 2026

Apart from any fair dealing for the purposes of research, private study, or criticism or review, as permitted under the Copyright, Designs and Patents Act, 1988, this publication may not be reproduced, stored or transmitted in any form, or by any means, without the prior permission in writing of the publisher, or in the case of reprographic reproduction, in accordance with the terms of licences issued by the Copyright Licensing Agency. Enquiries concerning reproduction outside those terms should be sent to the publisher.

Editor: Kate Keers
Editorial Assistant: Becky Oliver
Production editor: Sarah Cooke
Marketing manager: Maria Omena
Cover design: Bhairvi Vyas
Typeset by: C&M Digitals (P) Ltd, Chennai, India
Printed in the UK

Library of Congress Control Number: 2024949736

British Library Cataloguing in Publication data

A catalogue record for this book is available from the British Library

ISBN 978-1-5296-8226-7
ISBN 978-1-5296-8225-0 (pbk)

Contents

Acknowledgements

Huge thanks to Kate Keers from Sage Publishing for her excellent advice and support throughout the whole book writing process, from proposal to submission, and without whom this book would not have been possible. Thanks also to Sarah Cooke and Thea Watson for their support, helpful edits, and keeping everything on track. I would also like to thank Sahar Jamfar for her support and encouragement, and Becky Oliver for her hard work, support and friendly advice needed to complete this book.

I would like to thank my amazing colleagues from the University of Roehampton: Professor Adele Costabile, Dr Astrid Hauge-Evans, Jo Peat, Professor Jolanta Opacka-Juffry, Dr Kay Sharp, Dr Michael Patterson, Dr Olah Hakim, Dr Patrick Brady, Dr Simon Dyall and Dr Yvonne Jeanes.

I would like to thank all my students past and present, including Adriana, Bells and Jemma, for their engagement and enthusiasm that has inspired my teaching and informed this book,

I would also like to thank my family for their support and encouragement always.

About the Author

Dr Sue Reeves is the Head of Teaching and Learning within the School of Life and Health Sciences at the University of Roehampton. With over two decades of teaching experience, she has received awards for teaching excellence and has acted as an external examiner for several universities. Additionally, Dr Reeves is a Senior Fellow of Advance HE. Her research contributions encompass a broad range of topics within the field of nutrition, including the impact of dietary habits on obesity, coeliac disease, and the promotion of healthy and sustainable restaurant menus. Dr Reeves is also a member of the international Toybox Malaysia team, which has been awarded two grants from the Medical Research Council and whose research is aimed at fostering healthy behaviours among pre-schoolers and their families in Malaysia. Furthermore, she serves as an advisor for degree programmes in both Malaysia and Singapore. In addition to her research, Dr Reeves has co-authored two books, *The Study Skills Handbook for Nutritionists and Dietitians*, alongside Dr Yvonne Jeanes, and *Mastering Your Dissertation*, in collaboration with Dr Bartek Buczkowski.

Introduction

The Aim of this Book and What it Covers

This book aims to provide advice and support for all students through the entire undergraduate programme from day 1 to dissertation. It will help you go from taking notes and getting organised and being in control of your work, to writing essays and reports, and ultimately completing a final year dissertation.

Becoming a university student can be an amazing experience, but it can also be a little daunting, especially when you may be a bit unsure of what will be expected of you. You could be living away from home for the first time, or navigating a new commute, and then you are faced with a different style of teaching from what you are used to, and a variety of assessments such as essays, critical reviews, reports and annotated bibliographies, that you may not have come across before. This book aims to provide you with the guidance and reassurance you need in order to help you approach your academic work with confidence, and offers a source of support to ensure you do well.

Good writing skills are essential at university, since most of the assessments you take will include some form of writing. It will be important to be able to express yourself clearly and be able to convey your thoughts and opinions in all your written work. What is more, these skills are considered transferable skills, which means you can highlight them on your CV and they will be of benefit to you, not only now, but when you start to look for your first graduate job.

Studying at university is likely to include much more self-directed learning than you have experienced previously, and so it may take a little time to find out what works best for you.

This book offers support for your independent learning and a chance to learn the key skills that are needed before you attempt any written work, then applies them to the different forms of assessment. Finally, it considers how all the skills you have learnt and developed can be applied to the final year dissertation. In doing so this book aims to offer the guidance required to develop your writing skills and excel in your assessments, from the first essay to the final dissertation, and give you confidence in your own academic abilities.

You can read this book sequentially in order, and it has been organised to include an indication of the chronology of skill development that you will need as you progress with your university course. But equally you can dip in and out of this book at any time depending on which assessments you are working on.

This book has been divided into three parts. Part 1 will introduce you to the academic skills you need to succeed, Part 2 applies them to particular types of written assessments, and Part 3 is all about the final year dissertation. These are explained in more detail below:

The skills

The first part of this book is all about preparing to study at university. From getting organised and knowing how to engage and be an active learner, to learning academic skills such as referencing. Key concepts such as 'criticality' and 'plagiarism' are explained. You are also encouraged to take care of yourself and know where to get further support.

The written work

The second part looks at the different types of written assessments that you may come across whilst at university, such as essays, reports, and reflective writing, and highlights the differences between them, whilst providing guidance and top tips on how best to approach the different types of academic writing required.

The dissertation

The final part of this book aims to guide you through all the stages of the dissertation from planning and deciding on a research question, and developing an argument, through each separate chapter, from the abstract and introduction right through to the methods, results, discussion, conclusion and even the appendices. This section will also highlight the differences that may be found in dissertations in different subject areas.

A more detailed overview of the organisation and content of this book is provided in Table 0.i.

Table 0.i An overview of the organisation of this book

Section	Chapter numbers	Content
Part 1	1–7	Getting organised
		Being an active learner
		Reading critically (and keeping records)
		Academic writing and constructing academic arguments
		Referencing
		When to use AI and when not to use it
		Looking after yourself and asking for help
Part 2	8–14	Writing essays
		Writing reports
		Critical reviews
		Annotated bibliographies
		Reflective writing, blogs, social media posts, and first person writing
		Writing in exams
		Reviewing your feedback so far
Part 3	15–22	Getting started – aims, formulating research questions, ethics, and working with a supervisor
		Writing your introduction
		Completing the literature review
		Writing methodologies
		Planning the results chapter
		Discussions and conclusions
		Abstracts, appendices, editing and proof reading
		Preparing for a viva – including interviews, presentations, and posters

Furthermore, each chapter has a top tip from a student, a chapter summary, a check list of things to do, and suggestions for further reading, so it is easy to navigate and find what you need.

Whilst this book offers support for your degree-level studies, it is recognised that sometimes there are slight differences in the approach to assessments in different universities and according to the subject that you are studying. In this respect, this book is no substitute for talking to your course leader and knowing what they expect of you academically. However, this book will offer you support for the skills and assessments you are sure to face, including the dissertation, and other assignments that you may not have come across before, and provide a firm basis from which you can progress and even excel.

Finally, I hope you have a wonderful time at university and enjoy every minute of the experience. Hopefully this book will provide everything you need to develop and finesse your writing skills, and spur you on to succeed in all your assessments, from your first essay to your final dissertation.

THE SKILLS

Introduction to Part 1

Part 1 of this book is all about helping you to prepare to study at university. This includes getting organised and knowing how to engage and be an active learner, to learning academic skills such as referencing. Key concepts such as 'criticality' and 'plagiarism' are explained in detail, and the pros and cons of generative AI are presented. At the same time, you are encouraged to take good care of yourself whilst you are studying and be aware of the support available to ensure your well-being and academic success.

1

Getting Organised

Introduction

Starting university is a really exciting time. But when you have a new routine, a heavy timetable and you feel like you are juggling lots of different activities it can be a bit overwhelming. However, with a little bit of planning and organisation, you can start the academic year feeling prepared and ready for all that lies ahead. This chapter aims to help you plan your time at university, including your independent study time, whilst also taking into consideration all of your other commitments, to help you get organised and get ready for university whilst also becoming an independent learner.

Before you start university

If you have already started your university course, the next few paragraphs may be a little late for you so feel free to skip ahead, but if you are about to start, I hope the information below will be useful as you get ready for your first day at university.

Once you have accepted a place at university, you will probably be sent a welcome letter, an email or a link to online information detailing how and when you need to enrol and, very likely, information about any accommodation you have applied for. Keep this information safe, and easily accessible so you can check it regularly, noting all the key dates and deadlines for confirmation.

In addition to the welcome letter, you may get sent a reading list. Do check out the books and articles on the reading list and see if you can get copies from your local library. The books will have been chosen carefully to give you a taste of what is to come and to help you feel prepared for the programme you are studying, so do try to find the time to read them before your course starts.

Some universities offer pre-sessional courses, such as English for international students, or Advanced Maths/Programming for those choosing degree programmes that require a certain level of maths or computer knowledge. In some cases there may be courses to help you with general study skills to help make the transition to university easier. So do check out what your university offers and consider if the courses on offer would be helpful now you are getting ready to study at degree level.

What if I am not clever enough?

Everyone probably suffers from 'Imposter syndrome', or a feeling that you are not good enough, from time to time, even your lecturers, but don't let feelings of self-doubt get in your way. You wouldn't have been accepted onto the course if you didn't have the right qualifications and the lecturers didn't think you had what it takes. You earnt your place and have a right to be there. There might be parts of your course that are slightly more challenging than what you are used to, but there will be lots of support to ensure you can develop the skills you need to tackle those challenges. Talking about your fears can really help, and it is very likely that other students feel exactly the same way, so chat to them. In addition to your fellow students, there are lots of people you can talk to, your lecturers, your personal tutor and specialist academic support staff. They can all help you meet every challenge head on and produce your very best work.

On your first day at university

You will need to prepare for enrolment. Check you have received all the information you need to enrol. Most of the information you need will be sent via email, so check your inbox carefully to ensure you have not missed any important emails. Print any documents or take screenshots of the key information you will need to remember, so you can make sure you go to the right place at the right time.

Read the information carefully as you may be asked to present certain documents such as your passport, copies of certificates, etc., which if you forget could delay your registration. You will probably be given an allotted time to attend to complete your registration, so make sure you allow plenty of time to get there as it may take you a while to find your way around the campus and get to the right location.

You will be given a new university email address. It will be very tempting to continue using your personal email because you are used to it and have it set up on your phone, but you must use the university one. If lecturers need to contact you they will only use your university email address. Plus most universities have strong spam filters, so if you email your lecturers using your personal email it is possible your email will go straight into their junk folder and they may never see it.

Some universities will distribute the timetable on the first day of term, but many institutions will send you a personal timetable in advance so you can start planning when you need to be in university. Universities understand that many students have work, caring responsibilities or even long commutes that they need to plan and organise ahead of the start of term.

Planning your time is going to be essential as in addition to lectures, work and caring responsibilities, don't forget there will be other activities you need to leave time for such as independent study, as well as sports, social activities and time to relax. With a new timetable, assessment deadlines, work, sport, and everything else, you are certainly going to need some good time management skills.

Time management

Time management is an essential skill, and balancing your university work alongside all your other commitments is going to need some planning and organisation. Therefore, you are probably going to need some sort of planner. This could be electronic or paper, it could be a calendar or a diary, or it could just be a table you draw up yourself. Whatever sort of planner you choose, make sure you can see the days and weeks ahead so you can plan in advance, as well as for the day to day.

An example of a very simple planner you could create yourself is shown in Figure 1.1. You could make yours more personal and detailed, by dividing the squares into morning and afternoon sessions, or adding in set lecture times, making it bigger, etc., whatever works best for you and your schedule.

Week	Monday	Tuesday	Wednesday	Thursday	Friday	Saturday	Sunday
1							
2							
3							
4							
5							
Reading week							

Figure 1.1   An example of a simple term planner

Once you have your planner you can start plotting all the things you know you have to do:

- Add in when you have lectures
- Write down when you are working or have caring responsibilities or other commitments
- Next add all your deadlines for the assessments
- Now look for spaces in the planner, where you can work on those assessments and do some independent study
- Do also put in time for hobbies, exercise and socialising.

Having a term planner will help you recognise what you need to accomplish over the next couple of months, but you might also need to plan what you are going to focus on each week (see Figure 1.2). If you don't have a diary you could probably create something quite easily on Microsoft Word or Excel that shows the days of the week and even hours of the day. Once you have the lectures marked in, look for the times, such as between lectures, when you will work on assessments and do any required reading, etc.

You could even take your planning to the next level, by creating a list of what you need to accomplish each day; this could be a note in your diary or it could even take the form of a 'To do list' (see Box 1.1).

	Monday	Tuesday	Wednesday	Thursday	Friday	Saturday	Sunday
8am						Work	
9am	English lecture				Creative Writing		
10am	English seminar				Creative Writing		
11am				Tutorial			
12pm							
1pm			Netball match				
2pm	Discovering Literature			Intro Journalism			
3pm				Intro Journalism			
4pm							
5pm							
6pm							
7pm		Netball training					
8pm			Team social				

Figure 1.2 An example of a simple week planner

Don't forget to build some slack into your planning, as sometimes things don't go to plan: a lecture may over run, or a task takes much longer than expected. But if you ensure you have some space in your planner this will not matter. If it turns out that you don't need the additional time you have built in, you can always take an extra but well-earned break.

It can be difficult to get a routine established in the first few weeks of university, when there is so much going on. But having a planner or planners, will help you establish your routine and can help you stay on top of your work load and ultimately reduce stress.

Box 1.1   An example of a simple day planner/to do list

Date: *Monday 28 September*

Task to complete today:

1. *Meet personal tutor at 10am*
2. *Read the assigned chapter*
3. *Download the Powerpoint slides for the next lecture*
4. *Be at work by 4pm*
5. ....

Prioritising tasks

With so many plans and lists it could be easy to hop from one task to another and then feel like you are not getting anything done. One good way of prioritising tasks is to choose just one thing from your to do list that you want to complete, write it on a Post-it note and put it somewhere you can see it (Bregman, 2020). When you have completed the task, you can throw the Post-it note away and choose a different task from your to do list. This way you are focused on just that one task, and not worrying about the whole list at the same time.

You may find that you automatically categorise in your mind some tasks as being difficult and other tasks as being easy, and perhaps you are more likely to put off the difficult tasks. However, new research from Lai et al. (2023), investigating how people can best approach tasks, found that by grouping the tasks you need to do so that you do some difficult tasks first, followed by a few easy tasks, can result in you thinking about all the tasks completed as being in the same category, rather than two separate categories. This then decreases the perceived difficulty of all of the tasks. They termed this the '*easy addendum effect*' and found that grouping tasks can lead to greater persistence, can help you to get more tasks completed overall, and result in greater satisfaction.

Chunking

If you have been assigned a very large task to do, the sheer size of the task can sometimes be quite daunting. In cases like these, 'chunking' can help. Chunking is the breaking down of a large task into more manageable chunks. So, for example if you were assigned to read 80 pages of a book before the next lecture, you could break this down into a target of 20 pages a day for the next 4 days. You could even chunk your time. If you have a period of four hours to study, it can be hard to maintain your concentration over the four hours. But splitting this into smaller segments of time with breaks in between can improve your concentration levels and help you stay focused. The Pomodoro technique is based on this concept (Cirillo, 2018). The Pomodoro technique is where you work for 25 minutes followed by a 5 minute break. After doing this for two hours, you can then take a longer break. By breaking up the time in this way you are more likely to stay focused, and even with the frequent breaks, can actually be more productive.

Independent learning

Now that you are at university you may find you need to do more independent learning than you have been used to previously. Although you will have your lectures, seminars, laboratory sessions, and even tutorials timetabled, you will also be expected to do independent study, and as such you will need to take responsibility for your own learning.

Each module you study will be given a credit value, say 10, 20 or 30 credits, but something like a large dissertation module could be more like 40 credits. The credits represent how much studying is expected. If you are taking a 10-credit module this relates to 100 hours of study; some of this will occur in class, say on average around 26 hours per term, but the rest of the hours should be completed as independent study. If the module is 20 credits, then this relates to 200 hours of study, and so on.

Independent learning activities include preparing for classes, doing the recommended reading and working on assessments. At first you may be concerned that you are not working on the right things, but most university courses are set up to support you in becoming an independent learner and so will give you lots of direction to start with and then increase the amount of independent learning gradually. However, you can help develop your own independent study habits by making sure that you:

- Put aside time for study
- Organise your notes and know which work is for which module
- Check your reading lists and keep up with any assigned reading
- Ask your lecturers for clarification if you are not sure what you need to do

Where to do your independent study

Some students prefer to do their study at university in between and after lectures, in the library or computer suites, and this can be a good way of separating work and home. All universities will have computer rooms, some of which will open 24 hours a day. You might have a favourite coffee shop you like to work in, or you might prefer or need to work at home. Wherever you are working, you are probably going to need access to a computer and a good Wi-Fi connection. Your university may have laptops that you can borrow and, in some cases, funding that you can apply for to buy a laptop.

If you are working at home, try to designate an area where you can work comfortably; it doesn't have to be a separate study room, it could just be an area of your bedroom. Whilst it might be comfortable to work on your bed, you might find that you get easily distracted or sleepy. Ideally, set up a desk or table to work at, with a chair that is comfortable and supportive. Make sure the chair, table and computer screen are all at the right heights so you won't injure your neck or back, ensure your feet can reach the floor or use a footrest, and check the angles of your arms and wrists so you don't create strain. There are lots of online check lists for setting up a work station such as this one: www.hse.gov.uk/msd/dse/assessment.htm from the UK's Health and Safety Executive that can help you work safely and comfortably at home. Do also take regular breaks to walk around and loosen your joints as well as giving your eyes a rest from the screen.

Think about making your study space a place that you will be happy to spend time in and be productive in. Keep it neat and clutter free, throw away pens that don't work and recycle papers you no longer need. Psychologists believe that cluttered spaces can have negative effects on our stress levels, and that removing clutter can aid productivity (Sander, 2022). Adding snazzy stationary, pots for pens and a plant to brighten up your space can make it look more appealing and the greenery can also have a calming effect.

When you are working, remove all possible distractions, so this might mean putting your phone on silent, or putting it in a drawer out of arm's reach. Turn off the radio or television. You might think you can work whilst watching TV but realistically you are not giving the work your full focus. Save watching programmes for your breaks or as a reward for your hard work.

Organising your files

Even though you will do most of your work online, you are still bound to have lots of papers and handouts. Don't just add them to a pile on your desk, sort them out as you get them. It is probably a good idea to have a separate folder or box file for every module or course that you are taking; different coloured folders will make it easy to grab the right one for the right module. Label the documents as you receive them and organise them either into date order or by topic, using separators to divide the materials and to make it easy to find particular papers later.

You will probably be mostly working online but even here, you will still need to be organised so that you can find what you need easily and not spend hours searching for particular files on your computer.

Everything you have on your computer is saved as a file. When you save your files, make sure every file has a meaningful name that you will understand when you come back to it at a later date. Keep file names concise and avoid spaces, use '_' if you need to separate words. You may also want to include a date as this can really help with version control. Be consistent with the date format: listing the year first (e.g. 20240728 is 28 July 2024 in the format YYYYMMDD) can help you sort files chronologically.

Use online 'folders' to help organise your files. Again, make sure the names are logical, perhaps use a different folder for each module you are studying, a separate folder for documents like your CV and cover letters, and another folder for anything to do with your dissertation, etc. If some of your files are getting very full and this is making it difficult to find things, then add subfolders.

You should also consider where you are saving your work. If you are working on your own laptop then this is probably quite straight forward, though even here you should make sure you have a backup such as saving your work to a USB stick. However if you are working on a university computer check if you are saving it to the computer itself or the university network. Most universities will give you access to a cloud-based service such as One Drive. Saving your work to the cloud has advantages in that you should be able to access your files whether you are at home or at university and from all your devices. Even with access to the cloud, you should still have a back-up. A USB

17

stick or a portable hard drive can be very handy, but also easy to lose, so make sure you take good care of them, and like your computer is password protected, make sure your flash-drive is too. Dropbox is a file hosting service and another option for the storing and sharing of files. Another way of backing up a file that is particularly important would be to email it to yourself, so you can access it from your email system. With files being saved in different places, version control could be an issue so make sure different versions are dated or numbered, so it is clear which is the most recent.

You also don't need to keep every file forever! It might seem daunting when you look at the long list of files on your hard drive but at regular intervals go through your files and delete the obsolete ones. Perhaps organise your files by date so you can go through the oldest files first and delete those files that are no longer needed.

Your computer's desktop can be a good way of accessing frequently used files fast, but like your desk in real life, it can get cluttered very quickly. The files on your desktop can be organised by right clicking on the desktop screen. You can then move the file icons around by dragging them and dropping them where you want (you may need to untick 'auto arrange icons'). You can organise them alphabetically or by size, and you can even change the size of the icons themselves, too. When you no longer need the files, move them to a folder to keep the desktop clear and uncluttered.

If you are working on the internet, there are probably certain websites that you frequently use: creating bookmarks or using the history function can help you locate those websites fast. In the same way you can organise your files into folders, if you have a lot of bookmarks, you can organise these into folders too.

How many tabs do you have open on your computer at any one time? Having too many open could be slowing down your computer, even causing it to crash the browser. Closing tabs when you have finished using them will make it easier to toggle between the ones you do need open, but will also make it quicker to close down your computer at the end of the day.

You will also need to keep your online journal papers and references organised, but we will come back to this in Chapter 5 when we discuss referencing.

VLE

VLE stands for virtual learning environment and most universities will use a VLE platform for teaching and educational content. VLE's are particularly useful for online teaching but they are also used for in-person, face-to-face teaching as they are a good place to store all the relevant teaching materials you need such as lecture slides, reading lists, links to online tools, and in most cases they are where you will access quizzes, tests and upload coursework. Different universities will use different VLE platforms and these might include Moodle, Blackboard, MS Teams, or WebCT. Whichever VLE your university uses, log on early and check you have access to the right courses and modules – if you think there is anything missing contact your programme lead or your IT department. Practise navigating around the VLE to see what content is there. The content may change, lecture notes and recordings may be added or there may be important updates so do check back regularly. The VLE may also be used to communicate with students, send announcements and provide a space to have online discussions with your peers.

Asking for support

If you are still struggling to balance your studies and other commitments, do speak to your lecturers. You are sure to be allocated a particular lecturer as a personal tutor, who should be your first port of call. The personal tutor might have a slightly different title depending on your institution – they could be termed an advisor or an academic guidance tutor for example, but in all cases they are there to provide student support. Your personal tutor will help you to understand the university's systems as well as offer support with academic skills. It is important you communicate with them regularly and keep them updated on your progress. They may not always know the answers you need but they will certainly be able to direct you to other services and support such as the health and wellbeing officer, or the student welfare advisor, so there will always be somebody you can talk to.

Top tip from a student 1.1

At the start of the term, I make a list of all the hand-in dates for every assessment on every module. Alisa

---

Chapter summary

Even before you start university you can start getting organised, ensuring you have all the information you need to enrol, access to reading lists and timetables and the university's virtual learning environment platform. Take some time to create a planner for the term and even week by week activities, including independent study, think about where you will work, and how you will organise your papers and online files. But never be afraid to ask for help as your university will have lots of people who can support and guide you to achieve your best at university.

Check list

- Check you have all the information and documents you need to enrol
- Do you have a diary or planner?
- Fill in your planner with all your activities, not just lectures
- Find out what support is available at your university

Further reading

Cirillo, F. (2018) *The Pomodoro Technique: The Life-Changing Time-Management System*. London: Virgin Books.

Dalla-Camina, M. (2023) Overcoming imposter syndrome. *Psychology Today*. www.psychologytoday.com/gb/blog/real-women/202306/overcoming-imposter-syndrome.

2

Being an Active Learner

Introduction

Being at university isn't just about showing up, it is about engaging with the course you chose to study, and one of the best ways to engage with your course is to participate in active learning. Active learning will not only help you stay focused and involved with the content you are studying, but it can actually help your thinking and problem-solving skills as well as help you revise. This chapter will give you lots of ideas on how to be an active learner, on your own and with other students, and how to actively reflect on feedback, and even how to set your own learning goals.

What is active learning?

Active learning is learning though activities that require you to participate, explore the content of your lectures and think about and reflect on what you are learning. Listening to a lecture could probably be described as passive learning, but writing notes, highlighting and annotating them and then summarising them would be active learning. Active learning will not only help you stay focused and engaged, but according to Brown (2014) it can also help you develop higher-level thinking skills. With active learning, you, the student, are at the centre; you are not just receiving information, instead, you are exploring it and developing and extending your own understanding.

Bloom's taxonomy

You may have come across Bloom's taxonomy, which is a framework for education goals (see Figure 2.1). The pyramid of knowledge could be described as a hierarchy of cognitive skills that help students learn, from lower-level thinking at the base of the pyramid to higher-level thinking at the top of the pyramid, describing the stages through which students can obtain new knowledge and gain understanding, critique and develop.

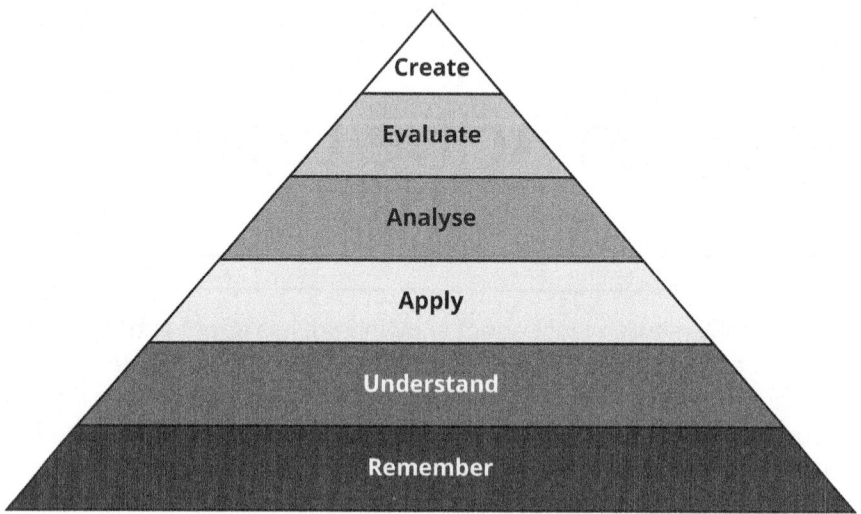

Figure 2.1 Bloom's taxonomy, adapted from Vanderbilt University Centre for Teaching (Armstrong, 2010)

Active learning requires the application, analysis and evaluation of learning materials, even the creation of ideas, all of which are at the higher levels of Bloom's taxonomy. That doesn't mean the lower levels are unimportant, as it is these layers that enable you to build on and develop your knowledge and skills.

Being an active learner

Your lecturers will probably try and incorporate in their lecture time opportunities for active learning such as laboratory practicals or seminar discussions, or they will use case studies and set tests, etc. to help maintain your concentration levels, keep you engaged with the content, and give you opportunities to explore the subject. There is some research that shows that students can only concentrate in lectures for periods of around 20 minutes, so lecturers are encouraged to break up their lecture time with different activities, discussions, videos and other activities including regular breaks to ensure the best learning gains for their students (Galindo, 2023). Likewise, when doing your own independent study, you should try to keep your learning active by doing different types of learning activities, as this will help with your understanding of the materials and keep you focused as you take a more in-depth look at your subject of study.

Active learning can include any variety of activities such as problem solving, summarising information, and doing quizzes. For example, if you just sit and read a book, you may find that you cannot remember everything you read and you didn't absorb that much of the content. But if you write notes and ask questions, and then later summarise your notes, highlighting key points, you will find that you retained a great deal more information – and that is active learning.

Try the following active learning activities:

- Write a summary of a book chapter you have just read
- Prepare for a presentation
- Complete a multiple-choice quiz
- Make specific flashcards
- Re-read your lecture notes, and use a highlighter pen to mark-up key points
- Draw a poster that shows a key concept
- Read a journal paper and make a list of key points
- Make a list of questions you have about a particular topic
- Go through worked examples
- Attempt a problem-solving activity
- Create an infographic

You don't have to be particularly creative with your active learning, even writing notes with pen and paper has been shown to help develop deeper cognitive understanding, and students report better recall (van der Velden, 2021). As such, taking an active approach to your learning is also a great way to revise for any upcoming tests and exams, where you will also find that by taking and annotating notes you will retain much more of the information than if you simply read your notes, and you will get a better understanding too. Practising and doing mock exams are also great ways of applying active learning to your revision process. But change it up from time to time: if you normally make lists of written notes whilst you read, try creating a visual mind map, or record an audio file, or simply switch to another subject or take a break.

Working with others

Active learning doesn't have to be a solitary activity: working as a group to solve a problem would be a very good example of using active learning. As a group you can discuss and understand different points of view and fully engage with the issue at hand. Contributing to class debates, and even discussing what you have learnt in a lecture with a friend could also be classified as active learning. You could even set up your own study group. Ask in class if anyone would be interested in establishing a study group, or if you are using a virtual learning environment such as Moodle you could put up a post on the online message board, or ask your lecturer to make an announcement in class. Think about what you want the study group to focus on: the lecture content, revision or problem-solving. Find a time that suits everyone's timetable such as between core lectures, and book a space to work; most university libraries will have rooms you can book that will have enough chairs and table space for everyone and even a computer linked to a screen, so you can all work together. Try to create an environment where everyone feels respected and supported. Study groups can be a great source of support, as other students on your course will appreciate exactly what you are experiencing as they will be experiencing it too.

Reflecting on your learning

Active learning might sound the complete opposite of reflective learning, with active learners being described as retaining information best when they do something active with it, and reflective learners preferring to think quietly about the information (Felder & Soloman, 2023). However, there is no reason why active learners cannot participate in reflection as an activity to help deepen their understanding. Reflection is an important part of the learning process, and is basically thinking about what you have done and then building on your experience so that next time you can do even better. Reflection can often help you make sense of complex situations or difficult pieces of work. You can reflect on feedback you have been given in person or on any pieces of assessment, to help you better understand what you did well and what you can do better next time.

There are many different ways of reflecting, and you should do what comes naturally to you, but there are some models that you can follow as you get used to reflecting on your work. Plus, the more you do it the easier it will become.

Probably the simplest technique is based on Schön's theory (1983), where reflection is divided into two types:

Reflection **in** Action and

Reflection **on** Action

Another way of putting this would be to say:

- Reflection whilst something is happening
- Reflection after something has happened

This could be thinking about something as you are doing it, say a presentation, or writing notes in a lecture. Then, later thinking about what you could do differently or what you could do to improve. Look at the case study in Box 2.1 below, and consider the reflection in action and the reflection on action.

Box 2.1   An example case study to consider reflection in action and on action

You are writing an essay that needs to be submitted by 2pm and it is already now 1.15pm – you are running out of time.

You realise if you add the references and proof read your work it will end up being submitted late. You decide to prioritise the referencing, forego the proof reading – submit the work on time.

– This is reflection in action.

Later, when you have more time, you consider what you could do differently if the same thing were to happen again. This might include:

- Starting the essay earlier
- Planning time in your weekly diary to work on the essay
- Doing your referencing as you go along
- Ensuring you leave time at the end for a final proof read
- Uploading your work on time

– This is reflection on action.

A more in-depth model of reflection is the one proposed by Gibbs (1998; see Figure 2.2). Although this one has six different stages, you may find it is more helpful for guiding you through the thought process, particularly if this is the first time you have tried reflective practice.

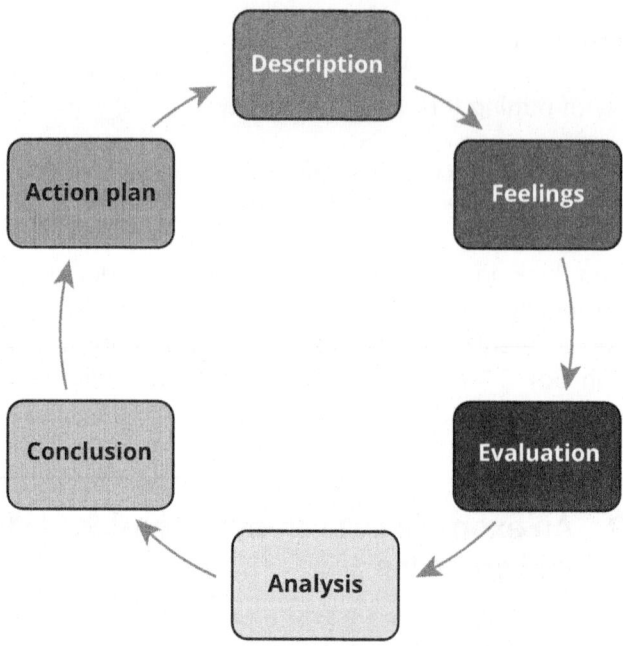

Figure 2.2 Cycle of reflection (Gibbs, 1988)

Briefly, the six stages of the cycle of reflection are:

Description – this is where you describe the situation or the experience

↓

Feelings – how did you feel about the situation and how do you feel now?

↓

Evaluation – what went well and what didn't go so well?

↓

Analysis – what do you make of the situation now; why did things go well or not so well?

↓

Conclusion – what could you have done differently; did you learn anything?

↓

Action plan – if faced with a similar situation, what would you do that would be different?

Essentially, reflection is a way of trying to make sense of your experience or turning something you find confusing into something you know how to handle next time. The cycle of reflection can be particularly useful to follow if you are asked to write a reflective essay, or if you are asked to reflect on a particular incident or something such as a placement in a school or a health care setting. Reflection is not just limited to your learning at university, it is something you may continue into your career, particularly if you have a career that requires continuing professional development (CPD), i.e. learning activities that support your job or role and ensure your knowledge is up to date. Reflection can help you make sense of your learning, and consider your strengths and weaknesses, in order to develop your practice.

Setting goals

When you are working hard and actively engaging with all your course materials, there may be times when you need to remind yourself why you are doing this, and having a goal can be very motivational. You are probably not studying for the sake of studying, you probably have a career aim in mind, and having long-term and short-term goals can be really useful in helping you see the way ahead in a step-by-step way. For example your long-term goal may be to be a doctor, or get accepted onto a Master's degree. But your short-term goal might be to pass the end of year exam, or to get better at writing essays. Your goals could be even more immediate, for example, when you sit down to study, you could think about what your goal is, and what you hope to achieve by the end of the study session – it could be to understand a particular concept, revise a particular topic, or write background notes for an essay. Having a focus can actually result in greater productivity, and less time procrastinating.

It is important to set your own goals, as they need to be personal, plus if you set your own goals you have ownership of them. Goal setting is also an important skill for self-management, so have a think about what you want to achieve and set your goals at the right level and the level you are at. For example, at the moment your goal may be to pass your biochemistry exam so you can get into the second year of your degree, rather than a goal to be Chief of Surgery (that can come later!).

SMART goals have long been part of the business world and were originally devised by Doran (1981) who thought that many business goals were too vague and not measurable, so he came up with the concept of SMART goal setting.

SMART is an acronym that describes a framework for setting goals and can be explained as follows:

S – Specific

M – Measurable

A – Attainable

R – Relevant

T – Time-bound

When you set your goal, make it **specific**: what exactly do you want to accomplish, and what actions will you need to take to achieve this? How will you **measure** your achievement: is there a metric or quantitative or qualitative data you can collect to show your progress? Make sure your goal is **attainable** and achievable, and that you have the skills and resources your need. Is your goal **relevant** and realistic: why is it important? And finally, what is the **time** frame for achieving your goal? Use the form in Box 2.2 to set out your SMART goal.

Box 2.2   An example of a SMART goal-setting form

My goal is to

....

Specifically, this will entail

....

....

I will measure this by ....

....

To achieve this I will

....

....

My goal is relevant because

....

....

The deadline is

....

Simply writing down your goals can help you define them and work through what you need to do, and then when you achieve your goal, you will feel a sense of accomplishment. Celebrate the win, watch a film, meet up with friends. Studying can be hard work so reward yourself for completing your goals. Achieving your goals will help build your confidence so you can aim for even greater goals in the future.

Use the study cycle to keep progressing

Keeping on top of all your studies can be hard work and there may be times when perhaps you feel you need a reminder of how to get it all back on track. The study cycle is a model developed by Frank Christ (1997) that outlines the stages of learning. When you are short of time or in a hurry it can be very easy to skip some of these stages so it is well worth reviewing them regularly. Figure 2.3 outlines the study cycle.

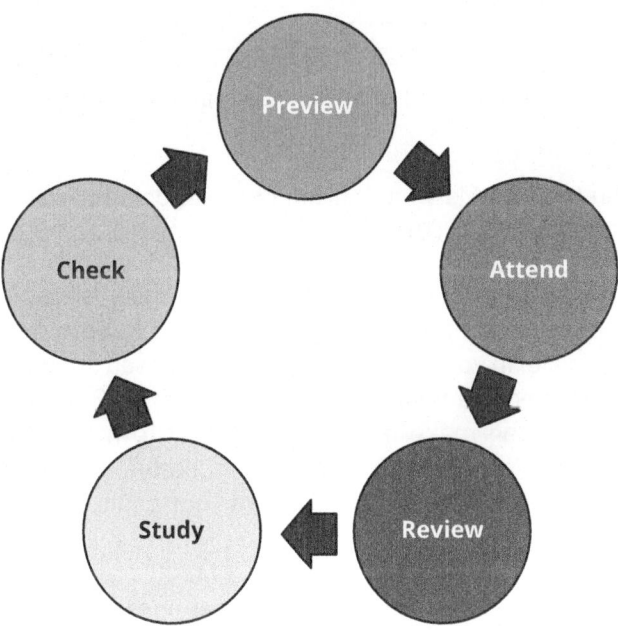

Figure 2.3 The study cycle (adapted from Christ, 1997)

The five stages of the study cycle can be described as follows:

1. **Preview** – before class go over the lecture notes, do any required reading and note down any questions you may have
2. **Attend** – don't underestimate how important it is to attend your lectures; watching a recording online is never the same as actually being present. Take notes and ask questions
3. **Review** – read your notes, fill in any gaps, highlight key points and summarise the main arguments

4. **Study** – arrange study time to work on problems, describe concepts out loud, find additional references and practise applying your knowledge
5. **Check** – create your own tests, describe the material to someone else, or attempt some past papers

You are probably doing lots of the points listed above already, but the study cycle links them together so the learning is more joined up and each stage builds on the previous one. Try applying the study cycle to each module that you are studying, or if you are unsure about it or are pushed for time, try using it for one module, and see how this compares to the learning and your progress on other modules.

Active learning takes effort

Active learning obviously takes much more effort than sitting and listening to a lecture, or reading a chapter. You may have heard the following quote:

> Nothing in the world is worth having or worth doing unless it means effort, pain, difficulty… (Theodore Roosevelt)

Whilst active study shouldn't be difficult and definitely not painful, it might take a bit more effort. But effort is related to your own sense of self-efficacy (belief in your own abilities) and has been shown in research to result in improved academic results (Chemers et al., 2001; Zimmerman, 2000). So if you can make the time and effort to make your learning active you will be rewarded not only with better understanding and remembering, but with the achievement of your goals.

Top tip from a student 2.1

One way I make my learning active is to use highlighter pens to pick out key points from my notes. This makes it easy to identify important bits of information when I come to revise. Leah

---

Chapter summary

Find out which active methods of learning help maintain your concentration and ultimately work best for you. This will ensure that you remain engaged with the subject you are studying, it will make it more interesting and will help you develop higher-level thinking skills. Use reflection to consider what you do well and where you may need a plan to improve, set SMART goals to help focus on what you want to accomplish, monitor your progress, and use the study cycle to stay on track and achieve your aims.

Check list

- Try out some different active learning activities
- Can you reflect on some recent feedback and create an action plan?
- Can you set yourself a SMART goal?
- Apply the study cycle to one of the modules you are studying

Further reading

Oakes, M. and Griffin, M. (2018) *The Student Mindset: A 30-item Toolkit for Anyone Learning Anything*. Carmarthen: Crown House Publishing.

3

Reading Critically

Introduction

You may have heard the expression that 'you read for a degree at university'. When someone says this, they essentially mean you study for a degree, but the use of the word 'read' certainly implies that your studies will include a lot of reading – and for most university courses this is true. But when you read at university you cannot just skim read or take every word at face value, you need to read in a critical manner. Critical reading will help you analyse the depths of what you are reading and by approaching your reading in a methodical manner it will also increase your understanding of texts. This chapter aims to explain how to read critically but also how to keep records of everything you read.

Reading

It is important you put aside time each week to do any required reading. In many cases you will be asked to read texts before class so you can contribute to group discussions. Try to read with purpose, so think about what you hope to get from the reading; is it for general background information, or specifically to make notes for an essay, or so you can participate in an informed debate, maybe even for enjoyment? Take your time when reading, perhaps scan the text first before reading it fully, and re-read as many times as you need. You may want to prioritise certain parts of the text, as some bits may be more challenging than others, for example if you are reading a scientific paper the results section may be more complicated than the introduction. If the text includes any tables and graphs do take time to look at these properly, it can be easy to skim or skip these, yet they may provide the key data or findings of the paper. Try to identify the key themes of the text and summarise them if you can. Sometimes you just need to give the material time to sink in, and then if you come back to the same text a few days later it will all seem much clearer. But reading critically is one of those things that the more you do the easier it will become.

Critical reading

The word critical will appear frequently in this book, but in an academic sense being critical is about assessing the evidence, considering different interpretations and arguments, and making evidence-based assessments; it doesn't mean being negative or nit-picking. When it comes to critical reading, this means reading with the purpose of a thorough examination of the arguments and explicit and implicit themes (Heik, 2022) in order to analyse, interpret and evaluate the text (Duncan, no date); these terms are explained below. The key differences between reading and critical reading are shown in Table 3.1.

Table 3.1 Differences between reading and critical reading

Reading	Critical reading
Reading	Analysing
Understanding what is written	Interpreting what is written
What does the text report?	What does the text mean?
Summarising	Evaluating
What information is provided?	What are the arguments and patterns, are there any underlying assumptions made?
Assuming the text is accurate and correct	Questioning and debating the information presented, recognising bias

Analysing

When we analyse a text we try to make sense of it, understand it, identify the arguments and recognise the patterns and techniques used. We try to find the key points of the arguments and try to compare and contrast.

Interpreting

When we interpret a text we try to understand what the arguments mean, and understand the methods that were used. This might include thinking about the context of the work, when was it written and where was it written, and how this may influence the author's views.

There could even be bias based on the period of history in which the work was written, or the views of the author at the time; there is more on bias below.

Evaluating

When we evaluate a text, we look to see if the views and statements are evidence based, if the work is logical, how it compares to other theories and beliefs, and furthermore, what are the strengths and limitations of the work?

What do we mean by recognising bias?

Bias could occur if an author has a strong view, shows favouritism, presents a one-sided argument, or is prejudiced. So when reading, try to ascertain if the writing is objective, and if it considers different perspectives. Are you presented with the whole story, or does it only represent the author's view of the world? Language is important so pay attention to the words that the author uses (and words that you use too) to ensure they are respectful and sensitive. Sometimes the language used can be loaded or exaggerated, perhaps to get an emotional response, or a claim that 'everyone else believes this so you should as well' (the bandwagon effect), so do look out for emotional manipulation (Gilmartin, 1999) as well as author bias in whatever you are reading.

Searching for relevant reading material

When looking for what to read, a good place to start would be the reading list for your module. Your lecturer may have given you this in class, it could be in a module handbook or on your virtual learning environment (Moodle, Blackboard, etc.). Some of the books and papers may be marked as core which will be essential reading, but there may also be further and optional reading for exploring further around your subject; start with the core texts first before expanding your reading. Before you buy any books check out your university library in the physical and online sense, since many libraries will have arranged access to e-books that you can read from your computer. If there is a book you think you will need a lot and perhaps use for several modules it might be worth buying your own copy; you may even be able to get a second-hand copy cheaper.

When you start to write your essays and reports you will also want to search for your own reading materials. Start by searching your library catalogue; you can also search Google Scholar. There will also be databases that are specific to particular subjects (your university library will have links to these from their own catalogue), for example:

Science subjects: Web of Science, PubMed, Science Direct

Arts subjects: Oxford Art Online, WorldCat, Arts and Humanities Citation Index, Cambridge Companions, Drama Online

Social sciences: EconLit, IBSS (International Bibliography of the Social Sciences)

Education: British Education Index, ERIC (Educational Resources Information Centre)

Languages: JSTOR, MLA (Modern Language Association International Bibliography)

There will be many other databases too. Do chat to your librarian as they will be able to direct you to the best catalogues and databases for your subject, and will help you find what you are looking for or help you request an inter library loan if they cannot access it.

When you find a good paper or book, it is always worth looking at the references that the authors used as they can lead to other good quality references on the same topic.

Keeping records

There are lots of reference manager software packages, e.g. Endnote, Mendeley, Paperpile, Zotero, etc. Some of these are free and some your university may subscribe to. They will also have guides on how to use them, and they will even offer training. These can save you a lot of time in the long run, so they are worth getting familiar with early on (for more on this see Chapter 5 on referencing).

By all means, create your own system for compiling lists of papers you have read. A table such as the one shown in Table 3.2 can be particularly useful if you are compiling papers in order to write a literature review, or an essay, as it can be a practical way of getting your thoughts together and organised in a logical manner before you start writing.

Table 3.2 Example of a method to compile your notes (in a table) to help with essay writing

Reference	Aim	Key points or results	Your interpretation

(Adapted from Reeves & Buczkowski, 2023)

How do you judge the quality of what you are reading?

You will be reading all sorts of publications as part of your degree, including journal papers, textbooks, monographs, review papers, specialist topic books, anthologies, newspapers, theses, online reports and blogs, field reports, and novels (depending on the subject you are studying). Being able to judge the quality and reliability of information is key to reading critically. But when there is so much material out there in the library, online and on social media, it can be hard to know where to start. The Meriam Library (2010) came up with a method that they call the CRAAP test. This is an acronym that stands for: current, reliable, author, accurate and purpose. Each word links to questions you can ask when trying to assess the reliability of what you are reading; these questions are outlined in Table 3.3.

Table 3.3 Using the CRAAP test to assess an article

CRAAP	Key Word	Questions to ask
C	Current	• Is the work current? • What date was the work published?
R	Reliable	• Is the work reliable? • Where was the article or information published? • Was it published in a peer-reviewed journal or online?
A	Author	• Who was the author? • Was the article written by an expert, or was it written by a public relations (PR) company?
A	Accurate	• Is the article accurate? • Is there any data or evidence for the points that have been presented?
P	Purpose	• What was the purpose of the article? • What audience was the article aimed at?

(The Meriam Library, 2010)

Journal papers

If you are looking for good quality information, journals are a good place to source your information since journals are a trusted form of communication, particularly scientific communication. In order to get published in a journal, the authors submit their manuscript and in most cases an editor will look at the work, but then the manuscript is sent out for peer review: this means it is sent out to other people who are experts in the same field who are asked to read the paper and write a review; this might include questions for the original author to answer, or points that need more detail, or general suggestions to improve the manuscript. The author then responds to the comments and if the peer reviewers and the editors agree the paper is worthy, it is published. In this respect when a paper is published in a journal the quality checks have already been done. That is not to say there is nothing left to critique – no research is perfect – but at least you know there has been a robust approval process.

Journal papers are also a really important source of information if you are looking for recent research in your subject area, as papers tend to get published more rapidly than, say, a textbook which could take several years from conception to printed copy.

Different types of journal paper

There are different types of journal papers and these are outlined in Table 3.4. Journal papers can be broadly divided into two types: primary literature and secondary literature.

Table 3.4   The different types of papers published in academic journals

Primary literature	Secondary literature
Original research papers	Systematic reviews and meta-analyses
Case studies or reports	Narrative reviews
Methodologies	Commentaries
Conference abstracts	Book reviews
Editorials	
Letters to the journal	

(Adapted from Subramanyam, 2013)

Primary literature: These are papers that include original research or information and can be described as follows:

- **Original research papers** – detailed research studies with a defined research question that report and present new work or data. Original research could

come in different forms such as an experiment, a survey, or a clinical control trial for example
- **Case studies or reports** – these report particular cases, often representing an individual, but they could be a place or a phenomenon (Tress Academic, 2019). These are more common in medical journals and often detail a particular disease with symptoms, treatment and prognosis
- **Methodologies** – describe a new technique or an advance on previous tests or procedures
- **Conference abstracts** – are short communications, sometimes just one paragraph but not longer than a page, to summarise new research that is presented at a conference
- **Editorials** – written by the editor usually to introduce a new journal or papers on a particular topic being published in the same issue
- **Letters to the journal** – these offer a response or feedback to a previously published research paper

Secondary literature: These are usually in the form of reviews that consider and summarise other research such as review papers.

- A **narrative review** – is a review of the literature that can be more descriptive and arguably more flexible than the other types of review
- A **systematic review** – attempts to identify, evaluate and synthesise all the empirical evidence that has been previously published and meets pre-specified eligibility criteria, in order to answer a specific research question
- A **meta-analysis** – could be described as a type of systematic review but essentially this incorporates a statistical technique used to combine data from many studies all written about a particular topic. The main reason for doing a meta-analysis is based on the idea that if you wanted to make recommendations you couldn't really do this from a single individual study, since the findings could be a one off. But by combining studies, you get more data, improve the accuracy of the original studies and the overall statistical power; for this reason meta-analyses are usually considered the highest form of evidence
- **Commentaries** – are usually just opinions on other research papers but they can provide an in depth response to the topic presented in an original research paper
- **Book reviews** – summarise and critique newly published books

Key points when critically evaluating a journal paper

When evaluating a journal paper, you can do this in much the same way you would any other article (see the CRAAP test, above). But many journal papers have a common structure. In the arts, a journal article may be more flexible but is likely to include the following sections:

Abstract

Introduction

Main body

Conclusion

References

Papers in arts-based subjects are probably less likely to have sections with data and results as such, instead they will present an argument, new observations or insights, or their views, which they will justify with evidence and explain.

In scientific journals, papers will usually be more structured and typically include the following sections:

Abstract

Introduction

Methods

Results

Discussion

Conclusion

References and or appendices

You can use the structure of the paper to help critique it.

The introduction should provide the background to the paper and why it was needed, but will also include an aim for the article. What is the aim of the paper, was the study needed, and would the study provide new insights? In the methods, you should always check who funded the study as this could introduce bias, for example if the study was on orange juice and the study was funded by a company that produces orange juice it's possible they have a vested interest in the results. Did the study get ethical approval? If not, was this appropriate (studies that involve humans and animals, or samples from humans and animals, need ethical approval). Were the methods appropriate or are there methods that would be superior? In the results section, try not to rush over the results: study the data and the statistical tests that were performed. Were they appropriate for the type of data presented? Then in the discussion section, you will see the data being explored. How was the data interpreted and put into context, were there any limitations to the findings? Finally, in the conclusion, do you agree with the conclusions of the authors? Some of these key points to consider when critiquing a paper are high-lighted in Figure 3.1.

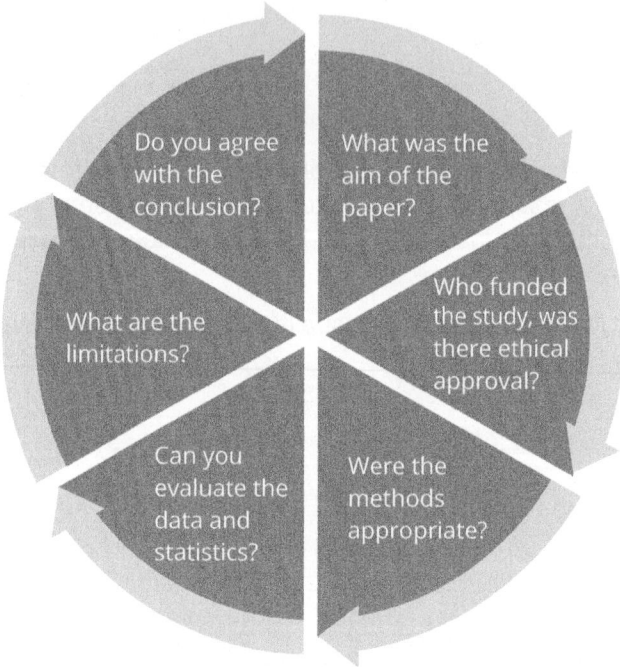

Figure 3.1 Key points when critically evaluating a scientific journal paper

Internet sources of information

Materials sourced through the internet have been described as the good, the bad and the ugly (Wallace & Wray, 2021), so it is always worth applying the CRAAP test to these sources, as described in Table 3.3. But how do you distinguish the reliable from the unreliable? Using the good, the bad, and the ugly analogy:

Good: is work that is reliable and includes peer-reviewed journal papers, e-books authored by specialists in the field or official catalogues and materials such as those published by museums

(Not) Bad: is work that would be fairly reliable and would include work that has been published prior to peer review, or unedited notes from a university academic

Ugly: materials from blogs, chatrooms, marketing information or content found on personal websites; best avoided for any academic work

Book and journal clubs

Discussing books and papers with friends can be a great way to help your understanding and appreciate different viewpoints. If your university has a journal club it would be worth going along, but if not you could always set up your own with other students on your course. Books and journal clubs can be in person or online, but the main thing is that they should be supportive and friendly.

Making notes

Notes are a useful way to document what you have read, highlight key facts, and your thoughts and feelings at the time of reading. If you have a paper copy of the article you are reading, you can highlight relevant sections, and annotate it by writing any ideas or observations you have in the margins. You can still do this with a pdf, by adding highlights and adding notes. Sometimes if it's an important paper you may still want to print it out so you can make manual notes (check copyright limits for photocopying for personal use). You can also make handwritten notes about any paper you read online. This can help you connect more with what you are reading and help increase your understanding of the paper. You don't just have to write your notes as lists, you can create flow charts as one idea leads to another, or get a large piece of paper and make a spider diagram to map out different themes and make visual connections (see Figure 3.2). You can draw in as many branches as you need, cluster similar information and use different coloured pens to highlight similar themes.

When writing your notes, try to summarise the key paragraphs, and comment on whether you think the writing and the ideas are 'good' and supported by the evidence or 'bad', perhaps supported by little evidence and even with some bias. But be careful when writing your notes that you don't copy sentences from the paper exactly as written, because if you then use your notes to write your essay you could end up replicating the same sentence and this would be plagiarism. Similarly if you are reading online, never copy and paste whole sentences from an online paper, because if it inadvertently ended up in your essay you would be accused of plagiarism; this is why it is really important to put your notes in your own words as you go along.

When you have finished, file your notes carefully in the relevant folder (online or a physical folder) so you can find them again when you need them.

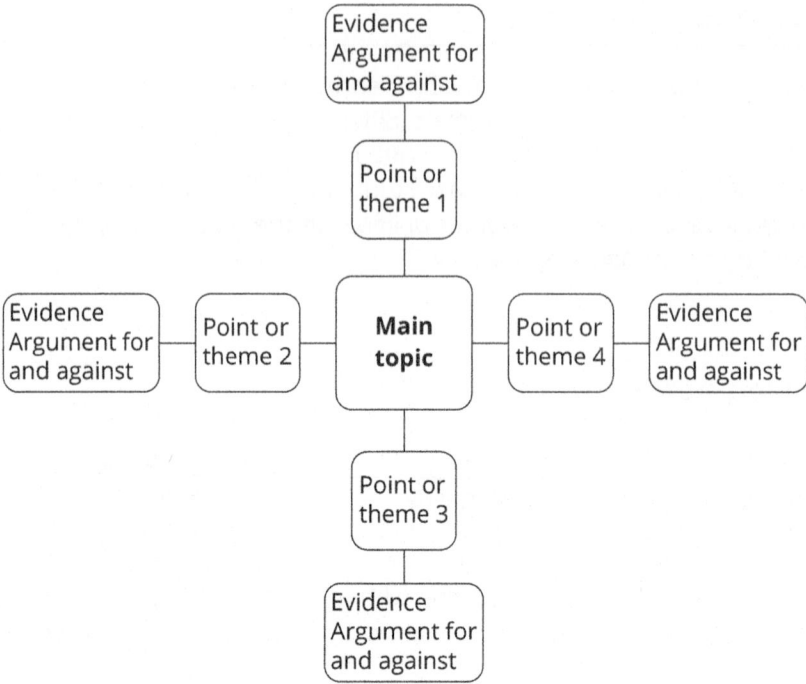

Figure 3.2 Organising your notes with a spider diagram

Top tip from a student 3.1

I try to read something every day, some days it is only one page, but I try to make reading a habit. Imani

---

Chapter summary

Hopefully you will now understand the difference between reading and reading critically. You will also have seen how important it is to be able to keep records of what you have read and are able to evaluate and judge the quality of what you are reading. Writing notes can help your understanding of what you are reading as long as you aim to summarise and evaluate as you go along, rather than copying exactly what you have read. As you will have seen, analysing, interpreting, and evaluating are key to critical reading.

Check list

- Try to read often
- Apply the CRAAP test to what you are reading
- Make notes about what you are reading in your own words
- Keep a record of what you have read

Further reading

Wallace, M. and Wray, A. (2021) *Critical Reading and Writing for Postgraduate Students*. London: Sage.

4

Academic Writing and Constructing Academic Arguments

Introduction

Writing skills are important at university since many of your assessments will involve different types of writing, and it is important to be able to express your ideas and knowledge clearly on paper. Academic writing also requires you to be able to debate and lay out your thoughts and construct an academic argument to bring depth and substance to your writing. But writing is not only a skill that you need for university, it is a highly transferable skill that you will rely on in the workplace. Being able to communicate clearly in writing is a skill much sought after by employers, so one well worth taking the time to develop and perfect.

Write regularly

The only way to get better at writing is to write regularly, and to keep on practising. Stephanie Meyer, the author of the *Twilight* books, stated on her website that she writes every day, even if only a page, and that she writes at night so there are less interruptions. Find your best time to write and try and do a little bit every day to make writing a habit; some days you may only be able to do a paragraph or two, but some days it will flow. On days when you feel like you cannot write perhaps you could write a list of things that you want to write and you can pick up your list the following day. However, if you have deadlines looming you might need to make a realistic plan for when you will work on your course-work, ensuring you have enough time to complete it.

Getting going with your writing

When you are looking at a blank piece of paper or an empty screen it can sometimes seem impossible to get started. But the best thing you can do is to write something. This could be a list of what you want to cover, your paragraph headings, or it could even be the first thing that comes into your head (otherwise known as a brain dump). You don't necessarily have to start at the beginning, if you have some good ideas for points you want to make later in the essay or report, you could write those down and then go back to your introduction later. If I am writing a scientific paper I often write the methods section first, as I find that section the easiest to write, then I do the other sections in order of preference, but I always make sure I have time at the end to go through the paper from start to finish to ensure every section of the paper all links up, is coherent and flows well. But the key thing is that once you have something written on the paper you can add to it, change it and delete as necessary; it will have got you over the starting line and then you can build upon it.

Another approach you could take if you are someone who finds it hard to get things down on paper but you could chat away on any topic, is to try talking to a friend or even yourself whilst recording what you say on your phone (obviously make sure you tell your friend what your plan is before you start recording). You could then transcribe what you recorded and then later go on to add more details and references as needed. Getting started is often the hardest bit, so anything that can get you to start putting words on paper is going to be good.

Whilst getting started may be the hardest part, never be afraid to re-work or re-write what you have written. You might be able to add details, or reword parts so that your message is more concise or clear, move sentences or paragraphs around so they flow better. Re-writing and editing is all part of the writing process.

Approaches to writing

People may approach writing in different ways. Some students prefer to write any old thing down on paper, then get more information and come back and edit it later (as in the brain dump mentioned previously).

However, other students prefer to make a plan. This could involve:

1. Reading around the topic and making notes
2. Highlighting your notes to indicate which information you want to include, perhaps numbering your notes in the order you want to add them to your written piece
3. Making a plan for the work – this might include paragraph headings
4. Writing a first (rough) draft
5. Checking where you need more information or details
6. Ensuring each section links with the next
7. Editing any spelling and grammatical errors
8. Writing your reference list; although you could leave this to close to the end, it is probably better to do as you go along
9. Reading through and checking your final draft
10. Submitting your work

After you have finished your work and you have received feedback on it, you might want to reflect on what worked well and what you could do differently next time to make the whole writing process easier in the future.

Writing style

The writing style that you need to use may depend on the piece of work. There is more information on this in Part 2, where there are chapters that describe the different types of written work, but some general guidance is provided here.

Firstly, you should consider who you are writing for. If you are writing for an academic audience you are likely to word this very differently than if you are writing an article for a magazine, or a story for young readers, so be sure to adapt your style to suit your audience accordingly.

Students often ask if they should write in the first person, where you put yourself in your writing, for example, 'I think that....'. If you are writing a diary entry, a memoir, or a reflective piece of work it would be very usual to write in the first person, e.g.: 'I felt that the work provided valuable experience of...'.

However in most academic work, and particularly if you are writing for a scientific subject, you should try to write in the third person, avoiding 'I' or 'you'. So instead of saying:

'I put potassium permanganate into the test tube and I stirred the mixture.'

You would write:

> 'Potassium permanganate was put into the test tube and the mixture was stirred.'

In scientific writing you are also aiming for a passive voice rather than an active voice, so:

> 'The mixture was stirred' rather than 'Stir the mixture.'

The only exception would be if you were writing a manual or a recipe where you are writing instructions for someone to follow, and here the active voice would be more usual.

Past tense

If you are writing a novel, although you can write in the present tense, it is more common to write in the past tense.

Present tense: Ajmal runs down the road.

Past tense: Ajmal ran down the road.

Scientific writing is usually in the past tense.

Present tense: Analyse the questionnaire.

Past tense: The questionnaire was analysed.

Try to be as clear and precise as you can in your writing and avoid generalisations. For example, if you did a survey of just two supermarkets say, Asda and Lidl, don't say you looked at supermarkets including Asda and Lidl, because this would imply there were other supermarkets included.

You should also avoid very general terms such as 'quite', for example if something is 'quite heavy', is it heavy or not? Could you add more details such as the exact weight, for example, to help quantify what you are stating?

Sentence structure

Technically sentences should have a subject, a verb and an object, or to put it more simply, a sentence should explain who (the subject), does what (the action, i.e. the verb), to whom (the object) (Hopkins & Reid,

2018). But essentially your sentence should stand alone and make sense. Try not to make your sentences too long and complicated with unnecessary words. Short sentences can sometimes be clearer but too many short sentences can also read a bit like a list and break up the flow of your writing, so try to get the balance right.

Reading your work out loud can really help with the clarity of your sentences, and help you ensure that each sentence follows on from the previous one. In this way use your sentences to build paragraphs, remembering that 'A sentence does not a paragraph make' (Anon), i.e., paragraphs should be longer than one sentence and contain more information than you could put in one sentence. However, rules can occasionally be broken, and sometimes in creative writing a one sentence paragraph is used to attract the reader's attention, give emphasis to a point, or perhaps to insinuate that something is urgent. Whilst an occasional one sentence paragraph is fine it is best not to overdo it.

Paragraph structure

Organising your writing into paragraphs is not only easier for the reader to negotiate your writing section by section, but also because they are a key way of structuring your writing. You should start a new line when starting a new paragraph and you should start a new paragraph every time you introduce a new idea or topic. If you are presenting a person or a character for the first time, or moving to a different location, then you should also start a new paragraph.

Each paragraph should also have a structure; you may have come across PEEL before. PEEL is an acronym for: Point, Evidence, Evaluation, Link. This can be quite a useful way of organising and explaining your thoughts:

- Introduce the **point** you want to make
- Show your **evidence** to support this view
- **Evaluate** and critique of the evidence
- Conclude your point and **link** to the next paragraph

However if you think this is too restrictive, you don't have to stick rigidly to this idea, but it certainly can help you start to prepare for academic arguments (more on this later).

Spelling and grammar

Whilst we don't want a focus on spelling and grammar to get in the way of your creative flow, the correct spelling and grammar is key to getting your point across in the way you intended and it is a key part of good writing skills.

Most computers have built in spelling and grammar checks and with apps like Grammarly it is now easier than ever to ensure your spelling and grammar are correct. So do make sure you are using the checks that you have at your fingertips. But it is often worth going back to basics to ensure your writing is presented in the best possible way.

Punctuation

Make sure you start every sentence with a capital letter, likewise for proper nouns (i.e. names of persons, places or things), and complete each sentence with a full stop, for example: '**T**ommy is visiting Birmingham on Friday.'

If you are asking a question, substitute the full stop for a **question mark** e.g.: 'What is the question**?**'

Exclamation points can be used instead of a full stop if you are trying to express shock or surprise!

Use an **apostrophe** to:

a. Indicate ownership e.g. 'Shirley's coat is blue'
b. Denote missing letters e.g. Isn't to mean 'is not'

If the words are being spoken, such as by a character in a story, or they are a direct quote, use inverted commas e.g. "All's well that ends well."

Colons can be used when you need to add further information: 'To cook pancakes you will need the following: flour, eggs and milk.'

Semi-colons can be used to connect independent clauses within a sentence, for example: 'Charlotte has gone to the ball; her sister stayed home.'

Hyphens are used to show the relationship between words e.g. 'check-in', or 'son-in-law.'

Commas can be used in different ways and essentially separate difference parts of sentences.

When speech is being presented, commas are used between the direct speech and the narration. For example:

a. Jane said, 'Do you have this in a larger size?'
b. 'Do you have this in a larger size?', she said.

49

After words or phrases that come before the main clause e.g.: 'However, research has shown…'

To add more information that perhaps could be considered an aside: '

My physics textbook, which weighs a ton, has some really great examples.'

When listing: 'The soup included onions, garlic, carrots, and coriander.'

And that brings us on to the Oxford Comma. **The Oxford comma** is when you add a comma to a list before the final and, to clarify a sentence that would otherwise be unclear. One example of this is: 'I have pictures in my room of my friends, Taylor Swift and Beyoncé.'

This gives the impression that the writer is friends with Taylor Swift and Beyoncé but adding the Oxford comma makes it clearer that it is a list: 'I have pictures in my room of my friends, Taylor Swift, and Beyoncé.'

However, some grammar experts think the Oxford comma is bad form and so it is sometimes seen as being controversial. Whatever your preference it is best to be consistent throughout your writing.

Abbreviations

These are frequently used for the names of organisations, or in scientific writing where there may be some very long terms that would be time consuming to write out every time. In these cases, the first time you use the term you should write it out in full and put the abbreviation in brackets, for example:

The World Health Organization (WHO)

Measurements were shown on a liquid crystal display (LCD)

From there on in, you can just use the abbreviation.

Constructing academic arguments

Most pieces of academic writing, including essays, reports and theses, will include some sort of academic argument. An academic argument is where you make a claim or present a particular take on a topic, and then debate the evidence for and against the point you are trying to make. Perhaps the word 'argument' could be misleading as you are not having a row or a battle, rather you are presenting evidence and providing reasoning for your argument. You want to ensure that your argument is both coherent and convincing (Wallace & Wray, 2021). So, you are not just voicing your opinion but presenting evidence to justify your point. For example, you could say: 'Young people eat a lot of fast food,' but this is just an anecdotal opinion. However, if you can incorporate and refer to relevant data you can show the reader how you are justifying your opinion. For example: 'The data from the Office for Public Health shows that there is a clear trend for young people to eat increasingly frequently at fast food restaurants.'

In this way it is clear to the reader that you have done your research and have found relevant evidence, in this case in the form of data, to back up your claim.

The evidence you present may not always be data, though this would certainly be common in the sciences; however in other subject areas your evidence could come from facts, published works, details from images, maps, or in some cases testimony, and if you were writing a reflective review it could even be your own personal experience (although please note that reflective accounts are different in this respect: your personal experience could be considered a source of bias in an essay or a report).

Most written academic arguments would follow a structure similar to that shown in Figure 4.1 and detailed below:

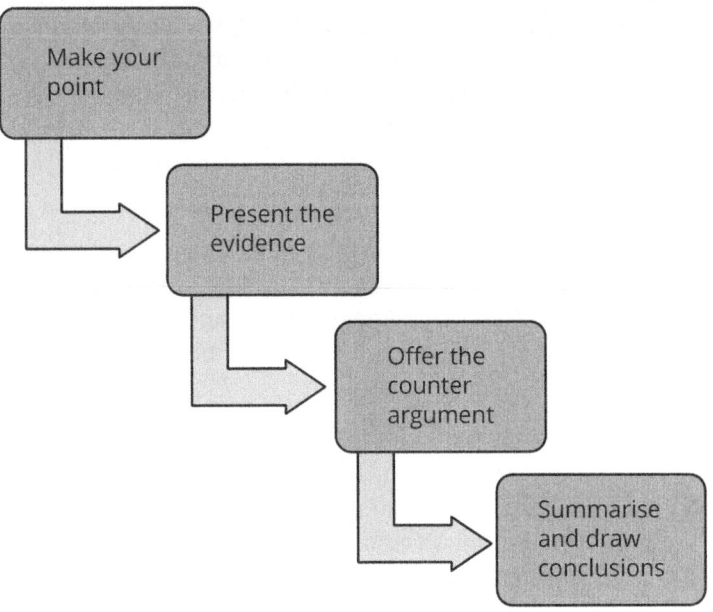

Figure 4.1   The stepwise structure of an academic argument

1. **Make your point**

This is where you state your point, or make a claim; this is a statement of what you are trying to prove and defend, so make it a strong argument.

2. **Present the evidence**

Here you should present your evidence to prove your case, it might be published work, data or examples that you can show as proof for your point.

3. **Offer the counter argument**

There could be objections to the point you are trying to make, so try to think what these could be, and consider the alternative viewpoints; what objections could someone have to your original point, and why might these arguments not hold up?

4. **Summarise and draw your conclusions**

This is where you summarise your findings and present a balanced overview of the point and consider the broader context.

Do make sure you avoid logical fallacies. A logical fallacy is where an argument appears to be true, and you may even have some evidence, but the evidence may not automatically be enough to prove your argument, so ultimately your argument could be false. A logical fallacy could be a deliberate attempt to try and persuade the reader, perhaps even playing on their emotions, but more often than not, it is based on weak evidence or flawed reasoning. To avoid falling into this trap make sure you have researched all the facts and your evidence is solid and reliable, making sure your writing is clear and unambiguous.

Do also try to be aware of your own bias. Whilst you might have a strong opinion on the point you are trying to present, make sure you don't exaggerate in order to get your views across, and do try to consider all the opposing arguments too, ensuring you are thoughtful and respectful of other viewpoints.

Good arguments are comprehensive and based on reliable evidence; they may be nuanced to show that you have considered all the angles and critiqued the data that you have, but they are never an all-out attack, they must be balanced and academic. Be as clear and specific as you can as this is how you will convince the reader of your point, as you join the academic debate.

> ## Top tip from a student 4.1
>
> *If I am worried that my writing is not clear enough, I read it out loud so that I can spot any mistakes and be sure it makes sense.* Princess

Chapter summary

When it comes to writing, the most important thing is to write regularly and preferably every day to practise this skill and improve your writing style. Spelling and grammar are important for communicating clearly and if this is not your strong point there are built-in grammar and spell checks, as well as apps you can use to get this right. Academic debate and critique are an important part of the writing process and you can organise your writing to make your point, present evidence and consider counter arguments in a structured manner to present a strong but clear argument. Putting your writing skills into practice, such as when writing essays and other types of written assessment, will be covered in Part 2 of this book.

Check list

- Find your preferred time to write
- Try to write regularly and ideally every day
- Do you feel confident you know which tense to write in?
- Can you construct an academic argument?

Further reading

Truss, L. (2009) *Eats, Shoots and Leaves*. London: Harper Collins.

5

Referencing

Introduction

Whether you are writing an essay, a report, a dissertation or any other piece of written work, you are going to need to use references. You will need to cite them in the text and then list the full details of every reference at the end of your work. This shows that you have done your reading, that you are basing your written work on published evidence, and that you are acknowledging your sources. It is essential that you reference any materials that you have used, and acknowledge the origins of your ideas, and referencing your work properly can also help you avoid inadvertently plagiarising. It is important that everything you write is written by you and in your own words so there is no risk of plagiarism. This chapter will help you get your referencing right and in doing so help you avoid plagiarism.

Referencing is a systematic way of acknowledging all the sources of information that you used to create your work. References should be used on all academic pieces of work whether they are essays, reports, dissertations or critical reviews; even posters and slides used in oral presentations should include references. References make it clear where you obtained the information that formed the basis of your ideas.

Referencing needs to be done in an organised and accurate way to make sure you keep track of every source that you used. You also need to record all the essential details so that your reader can locate any of the references that you have used.

Differences between reference lists and bibliographies

Reference lists and bibliographies are often thought to be the same thing, however there are slight differences. Reference lists only include articles and items that you refer to in your work; every reference cited in the text should be listed at the end of the work. However, bibliographies could include any information that you used to inform and write your assessment, including work that you didn't necessarily cite in the text but that you used for background reading. Annotated bibliographies are slightly different in that you also include an annotation for each reference, but more on that in Chapter 11. In all cases you need to ensure that you provide enough detail so that readers can find your references easily.

Citing work

Generally when you reference your work, you include a citation in the body of the text, and then provide the full details of the reference at the end of the piece of work in the reference list. When we say citation, we mean where you acknowledge your source in the text, and this is usually done either with the author's name, the work's year of publication, or a page number, or by using a number that relates to either a footnote or the list at the end, depending on which referencing system you are using. Some examples are given here, but see the next section for more about different referencing styles.

See below for different ways of citing a study:

- According to Dyer (2021) dress can be used to construct a chronological narrative of a national heritage
- Dress can be used to construct a chronological narrative of a national heritage (Dyer, 2021)
- Dress can be used to construct a chronological narrative of a national heritage (Dyer, p596)
- Dress can be used to construct a chronological narrative of a national heritage[1]
- Dress can be used to construct a chronological narrative of a national heritage [1]

Notice that there are five (if not more) different ways of presenting a citation and this is why you must check which referencing style you should use to make sure you are citing in the correct manner.

When citing studies, students often worry about when to use 'et al'. This is an abbreviation for the Latin word *et alia*, and essentially it means 'and others'. Typically you would use et al. when there are two or more authors that you want to cite, and where it would be too long to list every name, for example:

The following reference has six authors:

Collier-Sewell, F., Atherton, I., Mahoney, C., Kyle, R.G., Hughes, E. and Lasater, K., (2023) Competencies and standards in nurse education: The irresolvable tensions, *Nurse Education Today*, 125: 105782.

If you wanted to cite this journal paper in your essay you would cite (Collier-Sewell et al., 2023). The list at the end of your essay would be where you list all the other authors that are mentioned on the journal paper.

Referencing styles

As already mentioned, different subject areas do use different referencing styles, so do check with your lecturers which referencing style they want you to use. Although there are lots of different styles, they can be grouped as follows:

Reference systems that use a name and date citation:

- Harvard
- American Psychological Association (APA)
- National Library of Medicine (NLM)
- Chicago
- Modern Languages Association (MLA), though please note with this referencing system you cite the name and the page number rather than the year in the text.

Where the references are cited in the footnotes of the page, and there may be a bibliography:

- Oxford University Standard for Citation of Legal Authorities (OSCOLA) often used in Law for legal documents
- Modern Humanities Research Association (MHRA)

Where the references are listed in numerical order:

- American Medical Association (AMA) also known as Vancouver
- Nature

References written in different styles

Examples of how to reference a journal paper in some of the different referencing styles are shown in Table 5.1.

Table 5.1   Referencing journal papers in different referencing styles

Referencing system	Cited in the text	Reference list
APA	(Thomson & Wellmer, 2019)	Thomson, B., & Wellmer, F. (2019). Molecular regulation of flower development. *Current topics in developmental biology*, *131*, 185–210. https://doi.org/10.1016/bs.ctdb.2018.11.007.
Chicago	(Thomson, and Wellmer 2019, 185–210)	Thomson, Bennett, and Frank Wellmer. 2019. "Molecular regulation of flower development." *Current Topics in Developmental Biology*, 131, no.3: 185–210. doi:10.1016/bs.ctdb.2018.11.007.
Harvard	(Thomson and Wellmer, 2019)	Thomson B, and Wellmer, F. (2019) 'Molecular regulation of flower development', *Current Topics in Developmental Biology*, 131 (3), 185–210.
MLA	(Thomson, and Wellmer 185)	Thomson, Bennett, and Frank Wellmer. "Molecular regulation of flower development." *Current topics in developmental biology* vol. 131 (2019): 185–210. doi:10.1016/bs.ctdb.2018.11.007.

Books

Examples of how to reference a book in different referencing styles are shown in Table 5.2.

Table 5.2   Referencing books using different referencing styles

Referencing system	Cited in the text	Reference list
APA	(Bronte, 2012)	Bronte, E. (2012). *Wuthering Heights*. Penguin Classics.
Chicago	(Bronte 2012, 25)	Bronte, Emily. 2012. *Wuthering Heights*. London, England: Penguin Classics.
Harvard	(Bronte, 2012)	Bronte, E. (2012) *Wuthering Heights*. London: Penguin UK.
MLA	(Bronte 2012)	Bronte, Emily. *Wuthering Heights*. Penguin Classics, 2012.

There are other referencing styles, some of which are hybrids of other styles, or as Neville (2010) refers to them, 'horrible hybrids'. Some publishers, journals and even universities have their own styles, so it is always worth checking what style you are expected to use before starting to write.

Other sources

It is not just journal papers and books that you need to reference, you need to reference book chapters, websites, magazines, newspaper articles, census records, images, paintings, cartoons, government reports, blogs, podcasts, etc. Some examples of how to reference these are shown in Table 5.3 below, for these examples the Harvard referencing style has been used.

Table 5.3 Referencing different materials using Harvard style

Source	Reference
Chapter in book	Reeves, S. (2020) 'Current research in nutrition in the school curriculum', in Rutland, M. and Turner, A. (eds) *Food Education and Food Technology in the School Curricula*. New York: Springer, pp. 229–242.
Website	University of Oxford (2024) *Applying to Oxford*. Available at: www.ox.ac.uk/admissions/undergraduate/applying-to-oxford (Accessed 1 March 2023).
Picture	Van Gogh, V. (1887) *Sunflowers*. Available at: www.metmuseum.org/art/collection/search/436524 (Accessed 1 March 2024).
Newspaper	Foley, C. (2024) 'Paralympic Games: Donnacha McCarthy sparing no effort in push for Paris', *Irish Times*, 1 March, p.12. Available at: www.irishtimes.com/sport/athletics/2024/03/01/paralympic-games-donnacha-mccarthy-sparing-no-effort-in-push-for-paris/. (Accessed 1 March 2024).
YouTube video	Khan Academy (2016) Steps of glycolysis. Available at: www.youtube.com/watch?v=ArmIWtDnuys (Accessed 1 March 2024).
Email	Costabile, A. (2024) E-mail to Sue Reeves, 24 January.
Government publication	Office for Health Improvement and Disparities (2019) '*Healthy Ageing: a consensus statement*'. HMSO: London. Available at: www.gov.uk/government/publications/healthy-ageing-consensus-statement. (Accessed 1 March 2024).
Blog	West, F. (2022) 'How do heatwaves affect wildlife?'. Woodland Trust, 10 August. Available at: www.woodlandtrust.org.uk/blog/2022/08/how-heatwaves-affect-wildlife/. (Accessed 1 March 2024).
Film	*The Color Purple* (1985) Steven Spielberg [DVD]. Burbank: Warner Bros.

Direct quotes, paraphrasing and summarising

When citing work it is always best to put the information in your own words, it is not enough just to say where the words came from. To use an analogy, if you stole a dress from Marks and Spencer, but you told people it came from Marks and Spencer, it wouldn't change the fact you stole the dress! Simply put, always use your own words and cite your sources.

Only in very exceptional circumstances or if it is a famous speech or speaker should you use direct quotes. Where a direct quote is used do make sure you use speech marks to show the quote, and cite the source of the quote, for example:

'If everyone were cast in the same mould, there would be no such thing as beauty'. (Darwin, 1871, Ch. 19)

Rather than using direct quotes it is usually better to paraphrase, i.e. write in your own style and to use different words. However, don't just swop words around or be tempted to use a thesaurus to look for alternative words, as this can often change the meaning and lead to very a confused writing style. Instead, you want to show you understand the points you are making and can summarise what you have found. You could even combine information from several sources and write a summary of your findings and thoughts.

Keeping records

Some students like to do their references by hand, making a note of each reference as they go along, doing the references for one assignment at a time. However, you could create your own records, ensuring you have all the information you need to be able to reference accurately. You could decide to have a particular notebook where you jot down all your references, or you could create a table in Microsoft Word (Table 5.4) or a spreadsheet in Excel (Figure 5.1); you should use whatever option you are most comfortable with and will keep your reference records safe.

Table 5.4 Keeping track of your references with a Microsoft Word table

Author and year	Reference	Online link
What to cite in the text	*What to put in the list at the end*	*To find easily if needed again*
(Westbrooks et al., 2024)	Westbrooks, J., Low, D.A., and Brownlee, T.E. (2024) Determining the definition and components of successful soccer referee performance. *Journal of Sports Sciences;* 22: 1–6.	https://pubmed.ncbi.nlm. nih.gov/38389389/
Etc.		

	A	B	C	D	E
1	**Author**	**Year**	**Article title**	**Journal details**	**Link**
2	Westbrook, J., Low, D.A., and Brownlee, T.E.	2024	Determining the definition and componentsof successful soccer referee performance	*Journal of Sports Sciences*, 2024 Feb 22: 1–6	http://pubmed.ncbi.nl m.nih.gov/38389389
3					

Figure 5.1   Using Microsoft Excel to collate your references

Reference management tools

There are lots of online tools to help you reference correctly as well as manage your reference lists. Cite Them Right is an online referencing tool that provides tutorials for whichever style of referencing you require; the online content is based on a book by Pears and Shields (2022) that can also provide further information on the different referencing styles.

Microsoft Word has its own referencing system that you can find in the References tab on the toolbar at the top of the page. You can use this to add your references and compile the reference list at the end of the document.

There are also lots of different software packages to help you manage your references; some of the most common ones are RefWorks, Endnote, Zotero and Mendeley. There are also other reference management software programmes available but not all of them are free. It would be worth checking which reference management system your university recommends and has access to, as it is highly likely that they will subscribe to one of them. They will probably even provide resources and tutorials in how to use the reference management software too.

These packages can save your references directly from online resources and websites, help you organise your references into different folders, insert citations into your essays and reports, and then compile the reference list at the end; far quicker than doing it by hand.

Plagiarism

Getting your references right is one good way to avoid plagiarism. Plagiarism is the attempt to try and present the ideas and work of others as if they were your own (Hopkins & Reid, 2018) and it can be done knowingly or unknowingly (Osmond, 2016).

Whilst plagiarism can occur for many reasons, in many cases it is down to poor study skills. Common errors that can result in plagiarism, and how to avoid them, are summarised in Table 5.5.

Table 5.5 Common causes of plagiarism and how to avoid them

Reasons for plagiarism	How to avoid plagiarism
You didn't acknowledge your source	Make sure all information is referenced as you go along
Cutting and pasting text from an online source	Make sure you write all notes in your own words
Collusion	If you are working with a friend do make sure you write your work independently and separately
Unorganised notes	Make sure it is clear in your notes which are your own thoughts and which have been copied or taken from someone else
Self-plagiarism	Do not recycle any of your previously submitted work; write each piece of work from scratch, and where possible choose different topics and/or titles
Inaccurate citations	Keep detailed notes about each of your sources and make sure you only reference texts that you have actually looked at
You didn't use quotation marks	Although it would be better to paraphrase, if you do need a direct quote ensure you use speech marks and add a citation
You used an essay mill or got someone else to write it	It goes without saying that this is cheating and would be taken very seriously by your university

Detection software

All universities will have some sort of plagiarism detection software that will compare your work to published sources but also compare it to work that has been previously submitted through the software. Some of the plagiarism software programs can also detect the use of artificial intelligence (AI), so it is really important to ensure that everything you submit is written by you and you alone. Many universities use Turnitin as a portal for uploading your work for marking; the system will check for similarities and then the lecturers will mark the work, and you can see your marks and feedback through the same system. Penalties for plagiarism can vary between universities but a reduced mark or even a fail mark is a likely outcome. The fact that plagiarism can now be so readily detected really emphasises how important it is to write everything from scratch, in your own words, in order to maintain your academic integrity.

> ## Top tip from a student 5.1
>
> *I used to do all my referencing by hand but once I got used to RefWorks this was much quicker and saved me a lot of time.* Joseph

Chapter summary

Knowing how to reference correctly, by citing your sources in the text and providing full details in a list at the end, is an important skill that you will use in nearly all of your assessments, so it is important to get right. Once you know which style of referencing your university favours try to stick to that consistently. It is important to use your own words, paraphrasing and summarising information as you go, but if you do require the use of a direct quote ensure that this is clearly indicated as such with speech marks and that it is fully referenced. There are lots of reference management tools available, but whichever method you use to record your references, do make sure you always maintain meticulous notes to ensure your references are accurate and correct in everything you write.

Check list

- Find out which referencing system your university wants you to use
- Decide how you will keep track of your references: will you use a reference management tool or keep meticulous notes?
- Do make sure everything is written in your own words
- Upload your work to Turnitin to double check the originality of your work

Further reading

Pears, R. and Shields, G. (2022) *Cite Them Right: The Essential Referencing Guide*. London: Bloomsbury Academic.

6

When to Use AI and When Not to Use It

Introduction

Artificial intelligence (AI) seems to be everywhere at the moment, and its use is increasing. It can be tempting to use AI with your academic work, however there could be some strict penalties if you do. This chapter describes AI and generative AI in particular, and recommends that you find out what your university's policy on AI is. You should think carefully about when to use AI, and when not to use AI, to avoid anyone questioning your academic integrity.

What is AI?

Artificial intelligence (AI) refers to computers or machines that can think like a human and have capabilities that include reasoning and learning (European Parliament, 2020). This can include virtual assistants such as Siri and Alexa, search engines, face recognition and even driverless cars. AI tools essentially analyse big data and make connections through networks in a way that is not dissimilar to the way the human brain might, in order to give human-like answers when requested. An area of AI research that has generated much interest is generative AI, and one of the main reasons is because it has the ability to produce something new. Generative AI tools are based on large language models that can create text, computer code or even pictures (Marr, 2023). Because generative AI can produce new content it is easy to see why it is popular with students who can potentially use it to help with their writing, creating code, generating ideas or summarising large amounts of text or data (Chan & Hu, 2023). Some universities have even created assessments that require you to use AI. For example, at my own university, on one module, students are instructed to use ChatGPT to write an essay, and then critique the essay that is produced. So, they don't get any marks for the essay itself, instead the marks come from the students noticing where information is wrong or references don't align, and the overall critique of the essay (Dyall, 2024).

However, whilst using generative AI can be a great time-saving device, it could also be considered cheating, depending on the context in which it is used, and so it is important that you check your own university's policy on the use of AI.

Examples of AI tools

There are now an enormous array of AI tools available and this is growing daily. Some of the most well-known are:

Bing Chat

ChatGPT

Claude

Dall-E 2

GitHub Copilot

Google Gemini

Grok

Microsoft Copilot

Scribe

Some of the AI tools and platforms are free to use, whereas some of them have a fee or a subscription. The AI tool that you use may depend on what you need to use it for. For example, Dall-E 2 is used for image generation and image editing, and GitHub Copilot is frequently used for coding.

University policies and academic integrity

Before you even think about using AI you must check out your university's policy on AI, as these policies can vary widely. Some universities generally support the use of AI although they may have concerns relating to security, copyright and data protection. Other universities may be more concerned about academic integrity, and consider the use of AI that is unacknowledged as academic misconduct, and therefore this is penalised as such. There may also be exceptions, as sometimes an assessment may specifically ask you to use AI, but where this is the case it should be made clear to you. If in any doubt you should ask your lecturers.

How you can use AI

Some ways that you could ethically use AI include:

- To brainstorm ideas
- Provide revision questions, and then give feedback on your answers
- Summarising information to help you understand it
- Improve your spelling and grammar
- Debugging computer code

How it can be misused

Some ways that AI should not be used include:

- To write your essay
- For reflective writing
- Creating slides for a talk
- Manipulating images
- Fake videos or images
- Calculations (generative AI is generally not good at these)
- Writing anything that you want to pass off as your own

Generative AI is only as good as the data it has been trained on, and this can be inaccurate or even out of date. If there is not enough data available, AI can create hallucinations, which are essentially made up or wrong results. Then there is also the issue of bias. Bias can be introduced for many reasons including algorithm bias if the question is not specific enough, cognitive bias, since humans that input the data could unknowingly introduce their own biases, exclusion bias such as when there is missing data or important data has been left out, and stereotyping bias (Holdsworth, 2023). As such there is a lot of potential for inaccurate or misleading responses, so it is essential you check any outputs carefully.

Using prompts

To get the best out of AI you need to use the right prompts, and this is how you ensure you get the right content, but also the right tone and style (Peat and the AI Working Group, 2024; Siegel, 2024). When writing prompts you should always:

- Be as specific as possible
- Give a word count
- Tell it who it is being written for, e.g. if you want something written simply you could ask for it to be written for a ten-year-old; alternatively for something more in-depth you could specify for it to be written in the style of an academic journal
- If you are creating an image, consider the style in which you want it to be created – do you want it as a cartoon or a watercolour painting, for example?
- Consider whether you are using the right tool for the job: some generative AI tools are more creative, some are better for images, etc.
- Once you get an output, you can refine it further to get the exact output that you want.

If you are going to use AI

You should always critically evaluate any output, fact check the content, and verify any references. Refine responses by adding more questions and prompts with greater detail, even give examples of the sort of response that you want. Also ensure you safeguard your own personal data (including when you sign up), never give away passwords or financial information, etc. Likewise do not share any intellectual property including that of other people; this could include sensitive information, designs, patents or content of any kind (University of Oxford, 2024).

If you are using AI then you should ensure you reference this. You should keep a record of your prompts and the AI response by taking screenshots that you can put in the appendix of your work.

When referencing, the in-text citation should be as follows: 'ChatGPT-4 was used to generate ideas for possible projects (Open AI ChatGPT-4, 2024). A copy of the output can be found in the appendix.'

The information in the reference list should usually include which AI tool you used, the website address, what you used it for, e.g. to brainstorm project ideas, and the date it was accessed e.g.: 'ChatGPT-4 (2024) https://openai.com/chatgpt/, used to brainstorm project ideas. Accessed 30/5/2024.'

AI detection tools

In many cases your lecturer won't need a detection tool to know when you have been using AI, it will be obvious. You will be surprised at how many students don't realise that the AI style of writing is very different to their own usual style of writing, or they don't check for factual errors, or to see if the references are genuine. Sometimes they even leave in the prompts. However, there are several packages that can assess if AI has been used and offer a percentage score similar to that of packages such as Turnitin that check for plagiarism; in fact Turnitin also has an AI detection option. There are also lots of tools that your university may use such as Copyleaks, Content at Scale, Originality.ai, Winston AI and ZeroGPT. Whilst the accuracy of AI detection varies depending on which tool is used, you need to ask yourself, is it worth the risk? Penalties for using AI could range from getting a reduced mark, to failing the module, or worse if a repeat offence.

At the end of the day, don't you want to use the opportunity to practise and improve your own academic writing skills and submit work that you are proud of?

Top tip from a student 6.1

I was watching some presentations and it was really obvious that some of the other students had used AI, the references didn't relate to the subject of the talk at all, and I think the lecturers noticed this too. Nisham

---

Chapter summary

Use of generative AI is increasing. Whilst it is important to learn about AI, since it is used increasingly in the workplace, it is important to know how to use it ethically and appropriately. Ensuring you use the correct prompts and refine, critique and proof read the outputs is essential. It is also important to reference when you have used it, and know when not to use it.

Check list

- Check out your university's policy on the use of AI
- Can you create specific prompts?
- Do you know when it is appropriate to use AI and when it is not?

Further reading

Marr, B. (2024) *Generative AI in Practice: 100+ Amazing Ways Generative Artificial Intelligence is Changing Business and Society*. Wiley: Hoboken NJ.

7

Looking After Yourself and Asking for Help

Introduction

Going to university might well be the first time you are away from home for an extended period of time, and perhaps the first time you are responsible for organising your own time, preparing all your own meals and generally looking after yourself. Even if you haven't left home but are commuting to university you still need to look after yourself to ensure you are on top form physically and mentally, since juggling university, work and home life can be demanding at times. The changes to your routines and the challenges you face will be new for all students so to put you in the best place to meet these challenges head on you will want to make sure you eat healthily, exercise and rest well, but also know who to contact when things don't go to plan. This will help you perform your best and make the most of your time at university.

Eating well

Balanced diets are not about excluding particular foods, instead they are about ensuring you include lots of healthy foods to get the right amounts of energy, vitamins and minerals.

Fruits and vegetables are key to a healthy diet, and it's recommended we eat at least five portions a day. Try to have different types of fruit and veg with a mixture of colours to eat the rainbow and get a good variety of nutrients.

Carbohydrates: starchy foods such as rice, pasta, bread and potatoes are great sources of energy and can be good sources of fibre too, particularly if you go for the wholemeal varieties. Wholegrain foods are really important for the gut and enhancing the good bacteria that live there, which can influence digestion, metabolism and potentially even mood.

Protein: you will want some protein in your diet for growth and repair but also other functions such as hormone production and immune function, and fish, eggs and meat are all good sources. But there are also lots of plant-based protein foods such as beans, lentils and nuts (unless you are allergic) that you can eat if you are vegetarian or vegan; but be sure to eat a good mixture of different plant-based sources of protein to get the different amino acids that different foods contain.

Fats: yes, fats are also part of a healthy balanced diet and are important for fat soluble vitamins, but where possible look for unsaturated fats such as olive oil or the sort of fats you get in avocados.

Calcium: dairy foods can provide the calcium needed for strong bones and teeth, alongside other nutrients such as protein, iodine and B vitamins. If you cannot eat dairy foods look for plant-based alternatives that have been fortified with calcium and other nutrients.

Foods high in fat, salt and sugar: these are the foods that you should only eat in small amounts and include foods like crisps, biscuits and confectionary, that don't really contribute much in terms of nutrients. If you forbid these foods they instantly become more desirable, far better to have small amounts that you eat mindfully and really enjoy rather than going for an outright ban.

You can find lots more information on the British Nutrition Foundation's website. Furthermore if you have concerns around eating you can contact BEAT, an eating disorders charity, for information and support (see the Further Reading section at the end of the chapter).

Eating on a budget

If you are trying to eat healthily on a budget you will need to do some planning. Plan your meals and make a shopping list, and try not to buy too many extras. It helps to be a little bit flexible when shopping as sometimes there may be food on offer that you could substitute into your meals plans. Buying in bulk can be cheaper (but not always so check the price per gram), however check if you have freezer space or if there is a long shelf life on the product so nothing ends up going to waste. Food like lentils and rice are usually cheap and are good alternatives to more expensive grains such as quinoa. Nutritionally speaking, supermarket own brands and economy lines are no different to branded products

(Cooper & Nelson, 2003) so which you choose will come down to taste. Frozen and tinned fruit and vegetables can be cheaper and last longer than their fresh counterparts and also count towards your five a day. But choose those that are canned in natural juices, or have very low levels of salt and sugar. Seasonal fruit and veg is usually cheaper than other types and markets can be a great place to get fruit and veg cheaply.

Some universities have a food bank to help students who are struggling financially, and others offer a community fridge, where people can share unwanted food to avoid it being thrown away; find out what your university is doing to help students and also how they are reducing food waste.

Staying hydrated

The European Food Safety Authority (2010) recommend 1.6 litres of water per day for an adult woman, and 2 litres per day for an adult man, or around 7–8 glasses per day. If you don't like plain water, add mint, lemon, or other fruits to add flavour. Try to limit fruit juice to 150ml per day as juices and smoothies do contain sugar and can be quite acidic and therefore potentially harmful to your teeth if you drink too much of them. Similarly, it's best not to drink too many fizzy sugary drinks, and it is far better to switch to water. Likewise energy drinks not only contain caffeine and other stimulants, but they can also be very high in sugars too.

All drinks including tea and coffee can contribute to your water intake, but too much caffeine can cause other issues. Whilst you might like a coffee to help keep you awake and alert when you are trying to study, too much of any caffeinated drink will leave you feeling irritable and anxious and can disrupt your sleep patterns. In fact caffeine tolerance levels vary widely, while some people can drink coffee any time of day or night, other people might find a cup of coffee after 2pm means they can't sleep at night, or worse it makes them feel jittery, upsets their stomach or gives them heart palpitations. If this is the case it is sensible to avoid caffeinated drinks, especially since there are so many decaf alternatives now. Because of these varying effects of caffeine on different people it is difficult to say what the upper limit should be, but currently the U.S. Food and Drug Administration (2023) state an upper limit of 400 milligrams a day, which is about 4 or 5 cups of coffee, depending on the strength of the brew.

If you are rushing around to lectures and work you might not always have time to stop and get a drink, so carrying a refillable water bottle will mean you can drink regularly and stay hydrated throughout the day.

Alcohol

As well as directly affecting your health, drinking too much will disrupt your sleep and increase levels of anxiety, not to mention putting a large dent in your budget. So it really is important to consider how much you are drinking. There is no completely safe level of alcohol, however current guidelines recommend that no more than 14 units of alcohol are consumed a week, and this amount should be spread across three or more days, ensuring there are some days where no alcohol is consumed. In terms of units, one unit would be half a pint of low-strength lager or a small glass of wine, however many beers and wine have a higher percentage of alcohol and hence contain more units (NHS, 2024), so do check the label of what you are drinking. If you need support to reduce the amount of alcohol you are consuming please see the NHS website or contact your GP, especially if you experience any symptoms such as sweating, shaking and anxiety.

Think of ways you can socialise with your friends that don't include alcohol, such as the cinema or a fitness class. If you are going out drinking, plan ahead, set limits and a budget, and don't get dragged into rounds where you end up drinking more than you intended. Alternating alcoholic drinks with soft drinks is also a good way of reducing the amount you drink. Always watch your drinks and never leave them unattended. You can buy drink covers and testing strips to ensure they have not been tampered with, but most importantly you should look out for each other and always plan ahead how you will get home safely. For more on this see the Drink Aware website in the Further Reading section.

Exercise

The UK Chief Medical Officer (2019) recommends that adults should do some form of physical activity daily and do at least 150 minutes of moderate intensity activity, 75 minutes of vigorous activity or a mixture of both each week. In addition, they recommended doing strengthening exercises on two days and avoiding extended periods of sitting down; hence when you are studying it is important to intersperse this with physical activity of some sort.

Find something you will enjoy doing: join a social football league or take a Zumba class, you could do an exercise video on YouTube or just go outside for a walk. Any exercise is good exercise, but if you enjoy it you are more likely to want to spend time doing it. When you are studying hard it is so easy to spend a lot of time at a computer, so make sure you take regular breaks to rest your eyes as well as move your body.

Sleep

It is generally recommended that students should try to get seven to nine hours of sleep per night (Hirshkowitz et al., 2015), however it is the quality as well as the quantity of the sleep that counts. There might be lots of reasons why you are getting less sleep than you should: looming deadlines, too much caffeine, social activities, worrying about things, using blue light emitting electronics before bed, or generally a poor sleep routine. Getting enough sleep is important for general health and wellbeing and ensuring you are alert and can concentrate during the day.

Where possible try to establish a good sleep routine with regular sleep and wake times. Avoid caffeine in the evening, and alcohol, as that can also disrupt sleep patterns. It is also a good idea to switch off electronic devices an hour before bed. Try to establish a wind down routine, this might include a warm shower, gentle yoga or reading a book. When you get up in the morning make an effort to go outside and get some morning sunshine as this can really help if your circadian rhythm is out of sync (Harvard Division of Continuing Education, 2021). If it is other students in the halls of residence that are keeping you awake, perhaps talk to your flat rep or warden.

Medical help

Obviously if it is an emergency you should call 999 in the UK, 112 in Europe and some Asian countries, or 911 in the United States and in some other countries too, and state which emergency service you require. In the UK there is also a dedicated NHS website: 111.nhs.uk, where you can get immediate medical help for symptoms, injury, dental health, mental health, or support for an existing medical issue. But for other medical issues you will probably want to talk to a General Practitioner (GP). If you have moved away from home for university then you should register with a local GP and possibly even a new dentist as well. Don't wait until you have a medical or dental issue, do it as soon as possible. For common issues such as colds and sore throats you can also always speak to a pharmacist.

Dealing with stress

University can be a stressful time. You are meeting and living with new people, there are different routines, and deadlines and exams, so it is perfectly normal to feel stressed at times. However, if it is making you feel anxious and irritable and you find yourself worried, you should reach out and talk to someone. Your first point of call might be your university health and wellbeing advisor, or if you are not sure who to ask, speak to your tutor as they will certainly be able to point you in the right direction.

Some people find meditation or mindfulness helpful ways of dealing with every day stress. Meditation can help you clear your mind and focus, and mindfulness is a way of paying attention to being present, what is happening in the moment, reconnecting with what is happening and acknowledging whatever you are feeling at the time without judgement. Neither meditation nor mindfulness are quick fixes, but they might influence how we think about our feelings. There are lots of meditation and mindfulness apps or you can get some ideas for mindfulness exercises from the book by Mair (2019) listed in the Further Reading section at the end of this chapter. There are other useful apps, for example, Headspace is an app that can help you learn to meditate, which some people find can help them sleep better and help with stress. Your university may also have links for you to access some other wellbeing apps such as the Fika app. Like you would exercise your body, Fika is a mental fitness app that teaches you about techniques and tools you can use daily to train and prepare for the mental challenges we come across every day. Although anyone can practise meditation and mindfulness, they may not be right for everyone, if for example you have any mental health concerns, if you are suffering from the aftermath of trauma, you are dealing with grief or loss, you are experiencing psychosis, or you are depressed, you must get support from an appropriately qualified health professional (Mair, 2019). You should contact your doctor or GP who can help or put you in touch with the appropriate support straight away.

Asking for help

If you need help with anything, there is always someone at university you can ask. Probably on your very first day at university you will be assigned a tutor (though they may have slightly different titles at different institutions, e.g. personal tutor, academic guidance tutor, etc.). You will have regular meetings with your tutor and it is important you attend these, as they can help you monitor your academic progress, give advice on assessments and even career support. But you can also contact them when you need them, and let them know if you have any concerns. One of their most important roles is signposting other university services, so even if they cannot help directly they can always direct you to someone who can.

There will also be other people at your university whose job it is to support students. These can include but may not be limited to:

- Health and wellbeing advisors
- Counsellors
- Academic advisors
- Librarians who can help with study support
- Wardens of the halls of residence
- Head of College, or Head of Department
- Security
- Support for students with disabilities, learning differences and long term health conditions
- Medical teams including GP's
- Financial advisors that will have information on hardship funds and emergency loans, etc.

Check out your university's website to find out what support they offer. You may be surprised at quite how much support is on offer and the areas that this support covers.

If you are looking for emotional support and someone to talk to, particularly when the university might be closed, there are also other organisations you can call such as:

- The Samaritans offer a 24/7 emotional support and listening service. Telephone (UK) **116 123**
- London Nightline is an information and listening service run by students for students in the London area (but some other universities are also included) and their website is nightline.org.uk. Universities in other areas will also offer similar services https://nightline.ac.uk/
- Shout is a free, anonymous and confidential mental health text support service; text 'Shout' to 85258. They also have helpful resources on their website: https://giveusashout.org/
- Student Minds is a charity that can also offer support: www.studentminds.org.uk/

Please know that there is always somebody you can talk to, and your university will have lots of people who will want to listen.

Top tip from a student 7.1

My tutor has been a great source of support, even when they couldn't help me directly, they put me in touch with someone who could. John

---

Chapter summary

Hopefully you will have a wonderful time at university, and staying healthy will help you do that. Ensuring you eat a healthy diet, stay hydrated, and limit your alcohol and caffeine consumption, whilst also having good exercise and sleep habits, will be important. However, when things don't go to plan, there are lots of people you can turn to for advice and who can offer specialist support to help protect your physical and mental health. The most important thing is that you ask for help whenever you need it.

Check list

- Are you eating a balanced diet including five fruit and veg a day?
- Remember to grab and refill your water bottle
- Are you doing some form of physical activity daily?
- Think about how much caffeine and alcohol you drink – should you reduce this?
- Have you got a good sleep routine?
- Have you considered your mental health as well as your physical health?
- Do you know who to ask for help when you need it?

Further reading

BEAT (2024) Get information and support. www.beateatingdisorders.org.uk/get-information-and-support/.

British Nutrition Foundation (2023) A healthy balanced diet. www.nutrition.org.uk/creating-a-healthy-diet/a-healthy-balanced-diet/.

Drink Aware (2024) Drink spiking and date rape drugs. www.drinkaware.co.uk/advice-and-support/help-to-support-someone-else/drink-spiking-and-date-rape-drugs.

Mair, D. (2019) *The Student Guide to Mindfulness*. London: Sage.

NHS (2023) Student stress. www.nhs.uk/mental-health/children-and-young-adults/help-for-teenagers-young-adults-and-students/student-stress-self-help-tips/.

NHS (2024) Drink less. www.nhs.uk/better-health/drink-less/.

Summary of Part 1

Hopefully you now feel ready to study at university, and perhaps you have already started. The key skills you have learnt in Part 1 of this book, including how to be organised and set your own targets, looking after yourself, in addition to writing in an academic style and reading critically, should put you in good stead, and in the next part of this book we will consider how to apply these skills to different types of assessments.

THE WRITTEN WORK

Introduction to Part 2

Part 2 of this book looks at the different types of written assessments that you will come across at university, such as essays, reports, bibliographies and reflective writing. Each chapter will highlight the differences between the different types of assessments, whilst giving you guidance and top tips on how best to approach all your academic work.

8

Writing Essays

Introduction

Essays are a common assessment at university as they give you the opportunity to practise your writing skills, and the space to develop your ideas and understanding of a topic. It can sometimes be difficult to know where to start. But this chapter will describe how to analyse your essay title, explain essay structure, provide some guidance to help you explore your ideas and show you how, with a bit of research, you can organise your ideas and notes into an essay you will be proud of.

Understanding the essay title

The first thing to consider is the title of the essay. So before you even start writing or do any research make sure you fully understand the essay title. Read the title several times, out loud if that helps. Break it down and deconstruct it to ensure you know exactly what it means and so you are fully clear on what you are being asked to write about.

Most essay titles are divided into: key words, task words, and limiting words.

- The key words will be subject specific and tell you what the essay is about and what topics it will cover
- The task words explain what you need to do, for example 'describe' or 'compare'. Table 8.1 describes some of the most common task words and explains what they mean
- There may also be limiting words that set the boundaries as to what your essay should cover. One example might be if you were asked to focus on one of the UN Sustainable Development Goals: this makes it clear that your essay

should cover just one of the goals. Alternatively the limits could be written in a different way, for example if your essay asked:' How can we account for demographic changes in England during the eighteenth century?' then you know you need to limit your search to work related to the eighteenth century only. Alternatively, if your essay asked for 'recent research', then you need to ensure your references are up to date and are not too old

Table 8.1   Task words

Task word	Description
Analyse	Examine the different parts and how they may relate to each other
Assess	Evaluate and weigh up the information, judge the strengths and weaknesses
Compare	What are the similarities?
Contrast	Compare the differences
Compare and contrast	Show the similarities and the differences
Critically evaluate	Consider the strengths and weaknesses, and analyse and evaluate in order to make an assessment
Describe	Outline what this is like, and the key qualities
Define	List the key qualities, and state what is meant by them
Discuss	Consider different views and present the arguments for and against
Evaluate	Assess the importance of
Examine	Look closely at and in detail
Explain	Give a clear description or clarify why something happens or why it may occur
Illustrate	Use examples to explain; the examples could include diagrams
Outline	Identify the main points
Summarise	Provide a concise overview

Take a look at the essay title in Figure 8.1 and try to work out which words are the key words, the task words, and the limiting words. From the title, you can see that this essay is clearly related to anthropology, and on kinship in particular, as the subject key words are 'anthropology' and 'kinship' (and these are underlined). The task word is 'Describe' (shown in bold) so if you were writing this essay you would need to provide a descriptive outline of the key principles. The limiting word is 'four' (shown in italics), as it is clear that you are being instructed to describe four key principles.

Describe the *four* key principles of <u>kinship</u> in <u>anthropology</u>

Key

Bold = task word

Italics = limiting word

<u>Underline</u> = key words

Figure 8.1 *Example of an essay title*

Once you have fully understood the title then you can start thinking about how to answer the question and begin to do some research. But even after you have started writing your essay, do keep going back to the original essay title, as this will help you stay on track and focused.

Essay structure

Essays don't have a defined structure like reports do (see Chapter 9) but they should at least have the following:

Introduction

Main body

Conclusion

Reference list or bibliography

More details on these sections are provided below. From the list above it would be easy to think that writing an essay is a linear process with a clear start and end point; indeed some students like to work in this way, writing out the section headings and then listing subheadings beneath them, and this can be a very logical way to work. However, some people prefer to think of the essay structure as a circle, starting with the essay question or title, moving through the introduction, the main body, which can be organised into different paragraphs, and on to the conclusion, which should then come back to the original question, as shown in Figure 8.2.

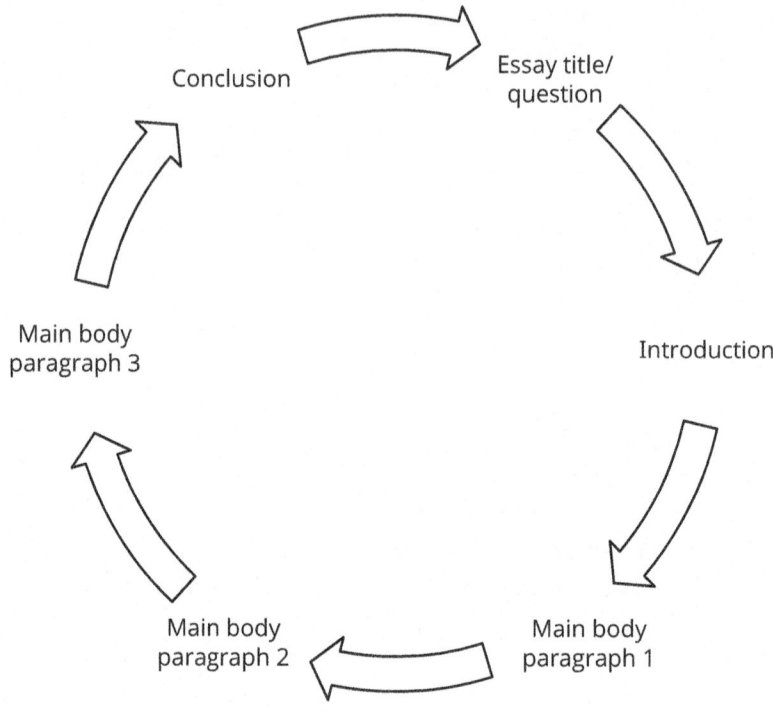

Figure 8.2 Circular essay structure

The sections of a typical essay are described below.

Introduction

The introduction will set the scene and essentially outline what the essay will cover; you may even want to use words from the title to emphasise that you are focused on the question being asked. Ultimately your introduction should try to grab the reader's attention so that they want to read more; this can be described as 'the hook'.

Just because your introduction is the first section to be read doesn't mean it needs to be the first section to be written, in fact in most cases you will want to write the main body of the essay first and add the introduction later.

Main body

The main body will vary in length and organisation depending on the essay, it can even be split into further subsections as required. By all means use paragraph headings to help organise the main points in your essay; you can always remove the headings later if you think they are disrupting the flow from one paragraph to the next. Each theme that you want to cover should have its own paragraph, and each paragraph should link neatly to the subsequent paragraph.

Each paragraph of the main body can be structured too. As mentioned in Chapter 4, the PEEL method is a good way of structuring your paragraphs. Remember PEEL stands for Point, Evidence, Evaluation, Link, whereby you: introduce your point, show the evidence for and against, evaluate the evidence, and link to the next paragraph. But don't let this structure be restrictive – you should present your evidence in the way that is most logical to you and thereby also the reader.

This is also where you are going to show your critique of the evidence, as critical analysis should be a key part of this section. Rather than just being descriptive, aim to show how you have engaged with the evidence, show your interpretation, highlight the significance of the work, or perhaps the failings of a particular theory, and evaluate the strengths and weaknesses, noting any limitations, and finally offer constructive suggestions.

It is perfectly fine to include diagrams and graphs if you think this adds depth and detail to your essay. But do ensure they are clear and neat, have a title and are referred to in the text as well. Also if they are taken or adapted from published work then do ensure this is clearly referenced.

You should also try to ensure that every paragraph in this section does link back to the original essay question, to make certain you are staying focused and not getting side tracked.

Conclusion

The conclusion is your final words on the matter or your verdict, so to speak. Essentially the conclusion should include a summary of your essay. You may also want to reflect on any limitations and highlight where further work is needed. The conclusion should also link back to the original essay question, and where possible answer the original question, so in effect your essay has gone full circle.

Reference list or bibliography

Whether you have a reference list or a bibliography, or both, will depend on the subject you are studying. Check the references are cited in the text as well as in the list at the end, and ensure you have presented all the details accurately.

Length of the essay

This will vary, and could be between 1,000 and 4,000 words, so you will need to check the guidelines you have been given carefully, as the number of words could also be indicative of the breadth and depth you will need to provide; a 1,000-word essay may be much more focused than a 4,000-word essay where you have much greater space to explore different arguments in depth.

You might have heard that a good essay should include three points, organised into three paragraphs within the main body of your essay. And this might be true if your essay is around 1,500 words, however shorter or longer essays are likely to need fewer or more key points respectively, so plan your essay taking into account the word limit you have been given.

Planning and researching your essay

In order to write an essay you are going to need to research the topic. However this does not mean you need to read everything ever written about the topic on which your essay is based. Taylor et al. (2019) recommends you should think about the essay before you do anything else. Think about what you already know, think about what questions the essay generates and think about the different ideas that you want to explore. Only then start to look for evidence in the literature based on your own specific ideas.

To help with your thinking, you could consider doing a mind map. This is like a brain dump but is arguably a bit more organised. Essentially it is where you start to jot your ideas down, and then try to organise them so similar ideas are grouped together. Then you can think about in which order you want to present these ideas and how your essay will flow through these different ideas. As you decide in which order the notes should go, you can begin to get a structure for your essay.

You can do your mind map on paper or computer. On computer it is easy to cut and paste your ideas and move them around the page as you begin to sort them into themes, and decide which order you want to cover them. If you are doing it on paper you can colour code your ideas, and have lines that connect them, or you could literally cut the paper with scissors to move your ideas up and down.

Once you have your main ideas sorted into themes, you need to start to look for evidence for those ideas and gather resources. You might start by looking at any lecture notes you have on the topic, as these are bound to provide leads and references that you can explore for your essay. But then you can start to look more widely at books and journal papers. Use search engines to find relevant journal papers. You might start with Google Scholar but then move on to look at the databases that are specific to your particular subject (there are more details on this in Chapter 3).

If you are searching online, you will want to make sure you are searching using strong key words. Take another look at the essay title and pick out the key words (as explained earlier). But also think about other words you could add to your literature search that will help you find relevant resources. Do consider alternative spelling, for example, if you were doing an essay on the role of dietitians in health care, you would want to search using the key word 'Dietitian' and the alternative spelling 'Dietician'. Some words are spelt differently in English and American e.g. 'color' vs. 'colour'. And some terms could be abbreviated e.g. 'LDL' rather than 'low density lipoproteins'. Try out different synonyms too, so for example if you were researching an essay on software developments, synonyms for software could include: 'application', 'program', 'package', 'code', etc.

You can combine different search terms using the Boolean operators And, Or and Not. (The name Boolean comes from George Boole in the 1800's who invented a form of logical algebra still used today for coding as well as searching; BBC Bitesize, 2024.) The Boolean operators are explained in Figure 8.3.

Operator	Description	Diagrammatic description
And	Combines search terms, so if you search for 'parrot AND fish' then the articles found would all include both of these words, so this could narrow down your search	
Or	If you search for 'parrot OR fish' the search will include anything that contains either of the words, so it broadens the search	
Not	If you search for 'parrot NOT fish', then you will only get articles about parrots	

Figure 8.3 Boolean operators to help you search the literature

(Venn diagrams adapted from University of Tasmania, 2024)

Make sure your search terms are not too broad as you could get a deluge of hits, but too narrow and you may struggle to find relevant resources. If you are struggling to find many papers on a particular subject but you have found one good paper, then have a look at the reference list they used, as this could lead you to other references that would be relevant, and those papers could lead to other papers too.

As you read, make notes in your own words summarising the main points, and noting down your thoughts and critique. Don't forget to make a record of each reference as you will need them later for your reference list or if you need to check your notes at any point.

Throughout this process try to stay focused, as it is easy to get diverted and start reading anything and everything, and this could be overwhelming. Instead focus on the question and the key points that you want to make in order to answer that question.

Putting your essay together

Start to put your notes together according to the structure you established using your mind map. But don't just put your notes one after the other, try to collate them and think about how they can link together smoothly. If several references are making the same point, summarise them rather than repeating the same information in slightly different ways, as this can look like you haven't read your own essay. If the references make contrasting points then highlight that too, remembering to critique the findings as you go. Add in examples and any further details and you will see your essay really taking shape.

You might also start to notice gaps, and here you may need to do some additional investigation to find some more relevant material, but it might also mean that there is a gap in the literature that you can highlight as part of your essay.

It is important that your essay flows, and there are common key phrases you can use to help organise your content and ensure your essay flows. Examples of these key phrases can be seen in Table 8.2.

Table 8.2 Common structure and linking phrases for essays

Common phrase	How to use it
This essay will...	As part of the introduction you can explain what the essay plans to cover and the aim
According to...	This can be a good way of introducing the author of a key reference
For example...	Use to introduce and further explain your evidence
To illustrate this...	Another way of introducing an example
Firstly, secondly... lastly	It can be really helpful to number some of the points you make as this can help retain a logical sequence through your essay
In light of...	Use when you want to refer to something that came to light because of other evidence or consideration
Prior to this...	A way of explaining work that has gone before or in the past
However,	Introduces an opposite or contrasting point; you could also use 'on the other hand'
Conversely,	Also used to introduce a new point that is the opposite to the previous one
Arguably,	When you want to make a point that you believe to be true but it cannot be said with absolute certainty
Furthermore,	Use at the start of a sentence when you want to add more evidence to your argument
In conclusion,	Use at the end of an essay to sum up; you could also use 'Ultimately'

Now you are getting close to the end and you can add in your introduction to the start, making sure you relate it to the original questions and set the scene for the points you have made in the main body of your essay.

Finally write your conclusion and summarise your findings, ensuring you have a clear 'take home message' that answers the original question.

Drafts

Providing you have the time, you can write as many drafts of your essay as you like. Your first draft might be quite messy but it is good to get your ideas into words and collate your evidence. Sometimes just calling your essay the 'first draft' can take the pressure off, as you can remind yourself that this is just the first draft so it doesn't have to be perfect.

Your second draft might be where you review everything and then realise that you need to move a few things around in order to make the essay flow better, and start to ensure all the references are present and correct.

Remember to leave time at the end of your final draft to proof read and edit your essay before submitting. Reading your work out loud can be a good way to check syntax and identify any wording errors. Finally, ensure your work is presented neatly with a clear font and line spacing.

Figure 8.3 summarises the process of essay writing, from understanding the title to the final submission, by organising the process into four key areas that you need to progress through: thinking, researching, compiling and finalising.

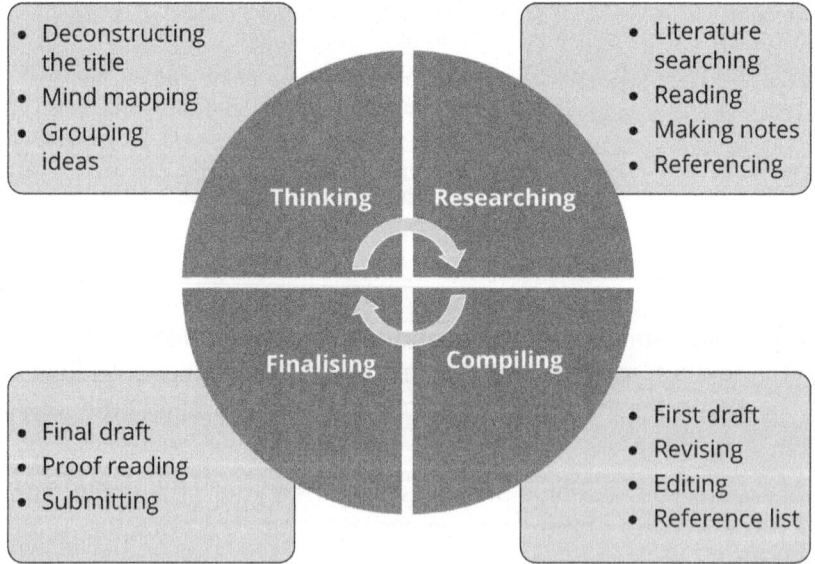

Figure 8.4 The essay writing process

Top tip from a student 8.1

Make sure you leave enough time to research and write your essay, sometimes it takes a lot longer to research the topic than you might first think. Harun

Chapter summary

Hopefully this chapter will help you feel more confident when you approach your next essay. Start by understanding the title, and begin to jot down your ideas as to what the essay is about, making notes and putting similar information together in order to get a structure for your essay. Researching and finding the evidence for your essay can still take time, but hopefully by thinking first, you can focus your reading, rather than trying to read everything and becoming overwhelmed. Write notes and structure these into paragraphs that collate and critique the information. If time permits, write several drafts in order to get your essay in the format that you want it, and so it flows from the introduction to the conclusion, allowing time at the end for proof reading.

Check list

- Pick apart the essay title to ensure you fully understand what you are being asked to write
- Brainstorm the title and write down all the ideas this generates
- Organise your information into themes
- Draft the main body of your essay
- Add introductions and conclusions
- Remember to check that you answered the original question
- Check your reference list and/or bibliography
- Save time for proof reading and editing

Further reading

Greetham, B. (2022) *How to Write Better Essays*. 5th edition. London: Bloomsbury Academic.

9

Writing Reports

Introduction

Reports are a very specific form of writing that require you to be factual, concise and formal. Reports are often used to present the results of research findings and in some cases draw conclusions or make recommendations. Reports are structured in that they are organised into different sections, which makes them relatively quick to read, and it is easy to find particular bits of information quickly (Cottrell, 2008). This chapter outlines the typical structure of a written report, to ensure you know what information goes into each section, and will also offer advice for using the most appropriate writing style to write your report.

If you are studying a science subject it is likely that you will be doing some laboratory practicals, and the findings and results from practicals are usually written up as reports. But other subject areas including business, law and other professional programmes will also ask you to write a report from time to time.

Reports are different from essays in that they are more structured, more concise and perhaps less discursive. Reports are often used in the workplace too (unlike essays) so being able to write a concise and structured report is also an employability skill you will want to perfect and may even want to highlight on your CV.

Before you start writing your report, always check the guidelines you have been given, as this will give you details on what the report should cover, and if there are specific data you need to include in the report such as particular graphs or tables. You should also check the word count, as this will determine how much detail you need to provide.

As with all pieces of work you need to consider who your audience is, and with a report it is likely to be people in the same subject or industry, so you can assume a reasonable level of knowledge. That said, your work still needs to be written clearly so it is readable and easy to navigate, and your findings communicated in a style suited to your subject area.

Reports are usually organised as follows:

1. **Title**
2. **Abstract or executive summary**
3. **Table of contents**
4. **Introduction**
5. **Methods**
6. **Results**
7. **Discussion**
8. **Conclusion**
9. **References**
10. **Appendices**

These sections are described in detail below.

1. The title

Titles should be concise but they should also be informative and describe the report accurately, so try to find the balance between being too brief and too wordy. Consider the report titles below:

The colorimetric practical

This title is too concise, and although the lecturer will know which practical you mean, the title doesn't really describe the experiment.

An investigation into the absorbency levels of six known paracetamol concentrations and comparisons to one unknown concentration of paracetamol using colorimetry

This title provides much more detail including the technique and what it was used for, but perhaps too many unnecessary words, for example are the words 'an investigation into' really needed, or does the title still work without them?

Colorimetric absorbency of different concentrations of paracetamol

This title provides relevant detail and describes the technique and what it was used for, but is still relatively concise.

Have a look at the titles of some journal papers in your subject area. You will probably find they are informative and descriptive; occasionally they may be humorous, but that could be a risk as not everybody has the same sense of humour. Ensuring your title is factual and makes sense is probably the best option.

2. Abstract or executive summary

Most reports for scientific subjects will require you to write an abstract. However in some subjects areas such as business you will be asked to write an executive summary. To some extent they are very similar; both will be presented at the front of the report and both will include a brief summary of the report being presented, and both need to be stand-alone.

An abstract for a report is usually around 100–200 words, and even if you were writing an abstract for a larger piece of work, say a dissertation, it should never be more than one page.

An abstract can be structured with paragraph headings, but more usually for a report it is unstructured. However, it should still reflect on the parts of the report including concise summaries of: the background to the report, the aim, the methods used, the results and a conclusion.

It is OK to put some key data into the abstract but it does need to be done very succinctly. You might have also noticed that there is no discussion in the abstract, since the abstract is a concise summary of the key findings and what they mean; comparisons with other studies and about the strengths and limitations can be read in the discussion section in the body of the report.

An executive summary, whilst similar to an abstract, may be slightly longer than an abstract and also include other information such as costings and recommendations. It is often written in a style suitable for decision makers and perhaps people who do not have time to read the full report. The executive summary should include a short introduction, and then concise summaries of each section of your report, ensuring these points are in the same order that they are in the report. Then you can make any recommendations, and finish with a brief conclusion.

In both cases, the abstract or executive summary will probably be the last section of the report to be written, since you will need to know what your results and conclusions are before you can succinctly summarise them.

3. Table of contents

Laboratory reports rarely need a contents page, since the sections of the report should follow the standard format. However, reports for business- or politics-related subjects always have a table of contents. The contents should list all headings and subheadings in the report, and so essentially outline the topics covered within the it, along with page numbers so each section is easy to find.

Microsoft Word can automatically create a contents page for you, see the References tab. This can be much quicker than typing out the list by hand, and it can automatically do updates if you need to move parts of the report around.

4. Introduction

The aim of the introduction is to set the scene for the report, and state the key issue being investigated. It will provide background information on what studies and research have been done before, and is essentially a short review of the literature, so you should use references here to support the information you are presenting. However, try to keep your review of the literature relatively concise and explain how previous work relates to your own, making it clear why there is a need for your report.

If you are writing a business report you could also state your 'Terms of reference' where you state who commissioned the report and why and what the report will cover, if applicable.

The length of the introduction will vary depending on how big the whole report is, but as a very general guide 15% would be quite standard; so for a 2,000-word report the introduction would be around 300 words.

The introduction culminates with the aim of your report, and your aim should set out what you are trying to find out from your investigation. You could also give your hypothesis here if you have one. The hypothesis will be a clear statement of what you predict will happen. So for a study looking to see if eating breakfast affects cognitive performance, the aim would be:

> The aim of this study is to investigate the effect of eating breakfast on cognitive performance.

The hypothesis would be:

It is hypothesised that breakfast consumption improves cognitive performance.

5. Methods

Sometimes called 'Methodology' or 'Materials and methods', this section is all about describing what was done, and as such should always be written in the past tense. A good methods section should include:

- The equipment that was used, including the name of the manufacturer and location e.g. gas analyser (Servomex, Crowborough)
- How the equipment was set up and calibrated
- The protocol that was followed
- The measurements that were made
- If you required any specialised computer software
- If you are reporting on a study that included human participants then you should state who provided the ethical approval (more information on ethical approval can be found in relation to dissertations in Chapter 15)

Describe everything listed above, and each step of the experiment, in as much detail as you can, such that anyone could follow your method if they were to repeat the experiment.

This section usually finishes with a brief outline of any data analysis or statistical tests that were performed on the data that was collected.

There might be rare occasions where the lecturer will provide you with the methods in order for you to complete the practical, and then rather than you just re-writing the methods, they give you permission to state something along the lines of 'Method – see the practical handout' (which you can put in the appendix). So do make sure you read the instructions carefully and listen to any advice that is given in the practical, and if you are still unsure, ask the lecturer.

6. Results

This section is for presenting your key data and so this usually includes at least one table or graph, and often more.

Check what data you are being asked to present. Sometimes you will be asked to include all the data collected during the practical in the results section. But often the raw data will be put in the appendix and

98

only the processed data will be put in the results section. This might require you to do some data analysis such as presenting the mean and the standard deviation of each group of data, or it could involve statistical tests to compare the data or to look for relationships.

Check how you have been asked to present the data. It would be unusual to be asked to present the exact same data as a table and a graph, usually it would be one or the other, as generally you should only present the data in one form rather than replicating it in different ways. But you might be asked to present the data in different ways to show that you know how to present the data in the best format.

Every table and graph should have a number and a title so that they are self-explanatory, but you should also have text that introduces each table and graph. However don't start discussing the results – save that for the discussion section.

7. Discussion

The discussion is for interpreting your data and explaining the findings, and here you can use your critical writing skills. This section could be split into 4 parts where you:

    i.   Summarise your results
    ii.   Compare your results with other studies
    iii. State the limitations of your study
    iv. Lay out what future work is needed

Once you have summarised your findings, critically evaluate your report and consider if the findings were as expected in light of other research that has been published, and you should reference the previously published work. If your results were different you could consider why this might be the case by comparing and critiquing your work and that of the other published studies. Perhaps there were limitations e.g. there was not enough data, the data was not representative, or there were methodological differences that may have affected the findings, so state what these were and what could be done to improve the study. Finish this section with suggestions for work that needs to be done next in light of the findings from your study.

8. Conclusion

The conclusion is where you summarise the findings of your report and show how they meet the original aim. If you are writing a business-type report, the conclusion may also include any recommendations that you want to make based on your findings. Resist the temptation to introduce a new point, as this section is all about final thoughts to end the report.

9. References

List every reference that you have referred to in the report here. Do check which style of referencing you should use; for a reminder of how to reference see Chapter 5.

10. Appendices

The appendices are for any additional information, data or graphs that you want to include that are not considered central to the report (Reeves & Buczkowski, 2023). This might include your raw data, your calculations and other documents that you needed to complete the study and write the report.

Writing style

Reports should be focused and concise so are usually devoid of flowery language. If you are studying a science subject, your writing needs to be as exact as possible so if you can include precise data or evidence you should. However, scientific writing could be considered very cautious, in that scientists tend to avoid making grand statements and use terms like 'in general' or 'the results appear to show', unless they can be 100% sure or can prove something with absolute certainty; even then they are likely to use the word 'theory' rather than 'fact', just in case a better theory that fits the data comes along later.

It is usual to write a report in the third person, avoiding personal pronouns. If you were describing how you collected your data using a questionnaire you might write: 'I created a questionnaire and I distributed it to all students in the class.' This could be re-worded to be in the third person as follows: 'A questionnaire was created and distributed to all students in the class.' To begin with you might have to really think about this and how to word each sentence, but it does become easier with time.

Generally reports should be written in the past tense, however there are some exceptions, as highlighted in Table 9.1.

Table 9.1 Which tense to use in the different sections of a report

Section of the report	Tenses used
Abstract	**Past tense** – because this describes the work that has been done
Introduction	**Present tense** when presenting general facts **Past tense** when describing previously published work The aim can be written in the **present tense** e.g. 'This study aims to…'
Methods	Always the **past tense**
Results	**Past tense**, unless referring to a graph or table, when you can use the **present tense**, e.g. 'Table 1 shows…'
Discussion	**Past tense** generally but you might use the **future tense** if you are making suggestions for future research/work
Conclusion	**Present tense** when making your conclusions. **Future tense** when discussing the implications of the findings

You will also want to ensure you are using a font that is clear and easy to read; Times New Roman, Calibri and Arial are probably the most common for a report, and do ensure the font size is large enough; 11 or 12 are recommended, though you can use 14 for titles.

Do use double-lined spaces as this makes the report look neater and is easier to read, and also leaves space for your lecturers to write their feedback. It is probably best to justify (ensure the edges are straight) the margins of your report; if you justify both the left and right this can lead to odd gaps in the middle of the lines so it is more usual to justify on the left side only. (In Word, you can change the line spacing and justification settings in the Paragraph section on the Home tab.)

Make sure you leave plenty of time at the end of your report to proof read it and check for errors. You will want to ensure that there is a thread that runs through the entire report, so a point made in one section is also referred to in the other sections. For instance, if you want to present results for a certain variable, let's say height, do make sure in the introduction you say why you are measuring height, then in the methods you say how height was measured, and in the discussion you discuss what the results of height might indicate; so the point you are making can be followed through from the start to the end of your report.

You don't have to write each section of the report in the order it appears in the report, you can write them in any order you want; perhaps to get going start with the easiest section. The structure that comes with a report also lends itself very nicely to goal setting (see Chapter 2), since you can set yourself the goal of completing one section at a time. Focusing on just one section of the report can make the task feel less daunting and much more do-able. Just make sure to leave plenty of time at the end to ensure each section runs smoothly into the next one.

Top tip from a student 9.1

When writing, I plan out the whole document with the main headings – this is a must for me as I need to see things coming together. Bells

---

Chapter summary

Report writing is a very specific form of writing that requires you to be factual and concise. Reports are structured, so a good way to get started with your report is to set out all the headings and then decide what information needs to go in each section. Then write one section at a time, but ensure you leave time at the end to go through the whole report and make sure there is a connective thread that runs through the entire report. Do take the time to check the presentation of your report, particularly any tables and graphs, as data are a key part of a report. The final section to write is your abstract or executive summary.

Check list

- Find out which referencing style you need to use for your report
- Plan the structure of your report and decide what information you need to put in each section
- Check you are using the correct tense for each section
- Find out if you need an abstract or an executive summary and make that the last piece of the report that you write
- Leave time for proof reading

Further reading

Hopkins, D. and Reid, T. (2020) *Write your Lab Report*. London: Sage.

10

Critical Reviews

Introduction

We have previously covered critical reading and critical academic writing, and this chapter on critical reviews will bring all those reading and writing skills together. A critical review requires you to read and examine a text in detail, but then also provide a written summary and evaluation of the text. This will really put your critical reading and writing skills to the test. But a critical review is also an opportunity for you to become an independent thinker and hone your critiquing skills before you start larger pieces of critical writing such as for your dissertation.

A critical review of a text

A critical review of a single text is a summary of the text but also an evaluation of the piece of work, and an assessment of what the work contributes to the field. The text you need to critically review could be a journal paper, or it could be a book, perhaps just one chapter or several chapters from a book.

To begin with consider why you are looking at this particular journal paper. Were you assigned the text, if not what made you choose this paper? If you are having difficulty deciding on a paper then consider the following:

- Have a look at any recommended reading you have been given; there could be some good suggestions there
- Make sure the paper is relevant to the topic you are studying
- Use online search engines such as Google Scholar, or academic databases to find an appropriate paper
- The abstract will provide a short summary of the paper, so use the abstract to check the paper is on the right subject

- If you find a paper on the right subject but it's not exactly what you need, have a look at the articles they reference for further inspiration
- Consider the quality of the paper; is it in a peer-reviewed journal, for example?
- Is it an original research paper or a review paper; original research papers will present new data whereas a review will summarise other papers
- Skim read the paper, to check you will be able to answer any questions you have been set as part of your assignment

After an initial skim read of the paper, it is a good idea to read the text fully all the way through so you have a good idea what the paper is about. If you have time, read it several times so you have a clear understanding of the paper. Make sure you read it in detail and don't rely just on your first skim read of the text. You might want to focus on one section of the paper at a time; some sections are perhaps trickier than other sections. For example, you may want to read the results section through more times than a section such as the introduction. Make notes as you read, highlighting key points, as this will help you when it comes to the writing of your review.

Critical review structure

The structure of a critical review can vary; in some cases you may be given set questions to answer, but a typical and general structure would be as follows:

- Introduction
- Precis
- Critique
- Conclusion
- References

These sections are described in detail below.

Introduction – this is usually quite brief, but should explain the topic that is being reviewed, and introduce the paper and the author. You may also want to state the aim of the paper or the aim of your review in particular.

Precis – this is a summary of the paper, and an overview of the important key findings of the paper you are critiquing, so even someone who has not read the paper will have a good understanding of what the paper is about. You should identify the key points or arguments of the paper, and you can even include a few examples to illustrate your points.

Critique – this is the heart of the review. Does the text contain a strong argument, is the argument evidence based, and is it clear and logical to understand or is it confused and meandering? You should highlight both the strengths and weaknesses of the paper. You may want to respond to the key points you have raised in the precis and critique these points individually; perhaps if you have space within your allotted word count, you could have a paragraph on each key point. You may want to comment on the methodology used, the validity of the findings or data, and any form of bias you may have found. You can use references to back up your own arguments. When critiquing the paper you can ask yourself a series of questions to help you get your thoughts together. Some possible questions are shown in Box 10.1.

Then consider, what does this text contribute to the literature on the topic, and what is your overall opinion of the text?

Conclusion – this is where you summarise the findings of the paper and your views of the paper; you may also want to highlight any further work that is needed, or questions that remain unanswered. Furthermore, if there are any recommendations on the basis of your critique you can present them here.

References – make sure you accurately reference the paper you are critiquing but also any other papers you referred to whilst critiquing it.

Box 10.1 Questions you can ask when writing a critical review

(Adapted from the Institute of Education Writing Centre, 2024)

1. What sort of paper are you reviewing?
2. What is the main topic?
3. What do the key results show?
4. How do the authors interpret the results?
5. Is the methodology appropriate?
6. Do the authors state any limitations of the study?
7. Is the argument a fair one?
8. Is there any potential bias?
9. How does this paper compare with other papers on the same subject?
10. What are your own views on the paper?

Writing style

Critical reviews are usually written in a formal style. However, do consider who the intended audience is. In most cases this will be for an academic audience, but if you were writing a critical book review for a newspaper or a magazine you will want to adapt your writing for the readership, depending on if they are experts or non-experts on the subject in hand, and possibly even the target age of the readers, for example a magazine aimed at young adults, etc.

It is always best if you write everything in your own words, to avoid any risk of plagiarism. If you do need to refer to text from the original article, say as part of your argument, do ensure you use quotation marks, so this is clear. For example:

> The author claims that blackjack is the only casino game that is beatable 'because blackjack is subject to continuous probability' (Mezrich, 2004).

Most of the time however, it is better to summarise or paraphrase the information in your own words. Summarising is where you review various sources of information, collate them in your own way and present them in your own words, although you do still need to acknowledge the references that provided the ideas. Likewise, paraphrasing is simply putting the information in your own original way, or restating information in your own words; as before you still need to reference the source of that information.

Comparing texts

There may be times when you are asked to write a critical review on two texts, or even several texts all on the same topic. Rather than listing a review on each, one after the other, the aim is more likely to be to compare and contrast the texts. In this case you should introduce each of the texts, but then you should try to highlight key points where the texts are similar and agree, and where the texts and arguments presented differ, before summarising. Some ideas for keys words to use to compare, contrast and summarise texts are shown in Table 10.1.

Table 10.1 Key words to compare, contrast and summarise texts

Where there is agreement	Where they differ	To summarise
Likewise	However	To summarise
Similarly	Conversely	To encapsulate
Analogously	Alternatively	To sum up
Correspondingly	On the contrary	Overall
Equally	In contrast	To review
Identically	Instead	To conclude
Complementarily	Nonetheless	Finally

Remember to critique all the papers, even if you personally agree with one of the texts more than the others. Your conclusion should evaluate the contribution each paper makes (Wallace & Wray, 2021) but also give your final judgement on the texts, and state if more research is needed.

Critical reviews of the literature

As you have seen, a critical review or critique is something that can be done to review and evaluate a single text such as a journal paper, or even compare and contrast several papers. However, learning to critique and writing a critical review is also great preparation for larger pieces of work such as a literature review. Literature reviews are an up-to-date synthesis of literature on a particular topic (Ferrari, 2015) and can be a standalone review paper, or even a chapter in your dissertation. There will be lots more on this in Part 3 of this book.

Top tip from a student 10.1

Choose your text carefully, some papers will highlight what the authors of the paper consider to be the strengths and limitations of their study and this can help with your own critique. Amir

---

Chapter summary

Critical reviews will bring all your critical reading and critical writing skills together. Whilst the structure for a critical review can vary, they typically have the following sections: an introduction, a precis (or summary), a critique, a conclusion, and a reference list. When writing your critique consider what questions you could ask and then answer, in order to pinpoint the strengths and limitations of the text, before summarising your views and highlighting further work that is needed. Once you can critique a single text, the next step is to compare and contrast two or more texts, and then you will be ready to put those skills further into practice in order to write a larger critical review of the literature.

Check list

- Carefully choose the text you want to review
- Is your review structured and does it include an introduction, precis, critique, and conclusion?
- Have you shown the strengths of the paper as well as the limitations?
- Are you writing in your own words, and summarising and paraphrasing as appropriate?
- Do you need to compare and contrast two or more texts?
- Are you now ready to write a longer critical review of the literature?

Further reading

Wallace, M. and Wray, A. (2021) *Critical Reading and Writing for Postgraduate Students*. London: Sage.

11

Annotated Bibliographies

Introduction

Coursework at university can vary, and you won't just be asked to write essays, you could be asked to write an annotated bibliography. An annotated bibliography is a list of references with a brief description and evaluation of each paper. This can be a good piece of coursework because it requires you to complete a literature search, identify appropriate resources, tests your referencing prowess, requires reading and note taking, develops your critiquing skills, and helps you learn a lot about a particular subject. Hence you are bound to come across an annotated bibliography type of assignment at some point during your degree.

How to go about an annotated bibliography

As mentioned in the introduction, an annotated bibliography is a list of resources you have read, but instead of just listing each item as a reference you annotate the resource, i.e. provide notes and a critique on each paper in a concise manner. An annotated bibliography can be a useful way of making notes on papers you have read, but it can be a piece of coursework where you are asked to write one on a particular topic, and therefore all the papers you select and critique should all be on that same topic.

When writing an annotated bibliography make sure you choose your articles well. You might want to show that you have read widely and should select your resources to show this. In scientific subjects you should aim to report on original research articles rather than review papers. Whether the paper is an original research article or a review is usually labelled by the journal, if the title doesn't give it away. But essentially an original research article will be a study in which new results or observations are presented by the author who actually did the study. Review papers consider multiple papers that have been previously published and summarises them. Table 11.1 summarises the differences between an original research article and a review paper.

Table 11.1 Differences between original research articles and review papers

Original research articles	Review papers
Primary literature	Secondary literature
Presents research conducted by the author	Based on papers previously published
Usually structured as follows: abstract, introduction, methods, results, discussion, conclusion	Structure varies but can include: abstract, introduction, main body and conclusion
There will be a short literature review in the introduction	The literature review will be the majority of the paper
Always includes a methods section	Most review papers do not have a methods section, although in some cases the authors may describe how the literature search was conducted
Reports new findings	Summarises and analyses existing research

Don't forget, as mentioned in Chapter 3, there are three different types of review paper – a brief recap is provided here:

1. A **narrative review** – a review of the literature that is descriptive and flexible
2. A **systematic review** – identifies, evaluates and synthesizes all empirical evidence previously published that meets pre-specified eligibility criteria
3. A **meta-analysis** – uses a statistical technique to combine data from many studies on a particular topic to provide a definitive answer

Once you have selected your papers, read each paper carefully ensuring you understand each section. You may need to look up certain words or do further background reading to fully understand the article. You should make notes on each paper, as you read, as these notes will form the annotation. For this reason it is important to write your notes in your own words and not copy the wording in the paper, to avoid the risk of plagiarism. The writing of the annotation needs to be kept brief, and should therefore be a succinct summary of what you have read. Your notes should comment on the key arguments and the strengths and limitations of the paper. It is usual to write in full sentences, but sometimes short phrases are permitted in order to keep the writing concise. Try to keep your notes factual and to the point as there is little word space for embellishments with this type of writing task.

In the science subjects a good annotation will include:

1. An accurate reference for the paper being reviewed
2. An introduction to the paper and topic
3. A description of the methods used
4. A summary of key results and if the results were significant
5. A critique of the study, including any strengths and limitations

In an arts-based subject, you will still need to provide an accurate reference, however you may need to summarise the paper and give your views, identifying and critiquing any academic arguments (there may not be any specific methods or results as such). In both science- and arts-based subjects, the critique of the paper is key.

As part of your critique, consider the methods used, the sample size, the reliability of the findings, risk of bias, as well as any strengths and limitations of the study. If one paper presents very different views to other papers you have read, you may want to highlight that too; as this will show the breadth as well as the depth of your reading.

In some cases you may also be asked to present your reflections on what you have read, your views on the article, or why you think it is a useful resource. This might be particularly useful if you are creating an annotated bibliography to write notes on what you have read for your own records, or as a method of synthesising information and learning about the topic.

An example of an annotated bibliography for a scientific journal paper is shown in Box 11.1. In this case the example has a word limit of 200 words. Box 11.2 is another example, this one based on a book, and in this case the word limit is 100 words, emphasising how important it is to check the word limits for your coursework. Word counts can vary and annotations can be between 50 and 300 words, so do check how much you are being asked to write before you start writing.

Box 11.1   An example of a journal entry for an annotated bibliography

Reference: Marques, L.R. (2021) Basal metabolic rate for high-performance female karate athletes. Nutrición Hospitalaria, Jun 10;38(3): 563–567. doi: 10.20960/nh.03390. PMID: 33749302.

Annotation: Karate is a type of martial art and is classified as an Olympic combat sport. Resting metabolic rate (BMR) is measured using indirect calorimetry and as such can be expensive and requires technical personnel so an equation is commonly used to measure BMR. However, there are many equations that exist, therefore the aim of this study was to investigate the applicability of different equations for predicting BMR in this population. The study was cross-sectional and included a retro-analytical component, to review the metabolic testing of 7 female participants measured using a Metacheck device. The results showed that only one of five equations tested, the Cunningham equation, was not significantly different to the results from indirect calorimetry, and therefore was suitable for use in this population. It is noted that whilst this study is the only one to consider the BMR of karate athletes, it only included 7 female participants, with a wide range of heights and weights, given the sports' varying weight categories, and that equations to predict BMR are not always accurate on an individual basis, and as such the application of this study may be limited.

Box 11.2   An example of a book entry for an annotated bibliography

Reference: Beard, M. (2017) *Women & Power: A Manifesto*. London: Profile Books.

Annotation: This book summarises two lectures given by the author that explored how ancient Greek and Roman history can be used to highlight the silencing of women in Western culture. Through a scholarly look at evidence going back centuries and through to modern day, she highlights the roots of misogyny and how powerful women have been silenced. The book is brief and some of the examples could have been developed further and with a greater number of references, however a strong academic argument for the redefining of power is evident throughout.

Typically each entry in the annotated bibliography should be listed alphabetically by the surname of the first author, like you would in a normal list of references, although sometimes you may wish to organise the entries in another way, such as by theme (Beatty & Cochran, 2020).

An annotated bibliography should be written in the typical academic style, with the focus on keeping the writing succinct and to the point. However if your annotated bibliography is for your own records, then obviously you can write as informally as you wish. But for any bibliography that will be submitted as coursework it is best to keep the writing style formal.

You need to be able to justify the books and or papers that you have chosen to include in your annotated bibliography, so select your sources carefully. Always aim to include journal papers and academic books rather than websites. Every item on your list should be of suitable quality, written by credible sources, and cover all the key issues relevant to the topic you are researching or have been assigned. Together, all the entries in your annotated bibliography should provide a comprehensive summary of the literature.

Marking of annotated bibliographies

If your annotated bibliography is for coursework, do make sure you look at how it will be marked, as it may be marked quite differently to an essay, for example. Although marking criteria may vary, there might be marks for each entry in the bibliography and each entry might include marks for:

- The selection of each paper – are they all relevant papers, and are they original studies?
- The study details – did you include an introductory sentence, were the methods described, what were the results, and were they significant?
- Your critique – have you noted the key arguments and any strengths and limitations to the study?
- There could even be marks for presentation, clarity and keeping to the word limit

---

Top tip from a student 11.1

It's important to pick the right sort of papers, original research studies rather than review papers, as this means you can critique the methods and results that are presented. Magda

---

Chapter summary

An annotated bibliography can be a good way of making notes on papers and books you have read, but it can also be a piece of written coursework, where you summarise and critique resources in a succinct manner. It is important to ensure you reference accurately, describe and acknowledge the strengths and limitations of what you have read, and ensure you keep to the word limits if you want to get good marks. But in addition, an annotated bibliography can be an excellent way of getting to know the literature in a particular area of study.

Check list

- Find out how many entries you need to present
- Choose your papers wisely
- Check you have reported the reference accurately
- Have you critiqued the papers you are presenting?

Further reading

Beatty, L. and Cochran, C.A. (2020) *Writing the Annotated Bibliography: A Guide for Students and Researchers*. Abingdon: Routledge.

12

Reflective Writing, Blogs, Social Media Posts

Introduction

You may be asked to do all different types of writing whilst at university and not always formal essays. Reflective writing, blogs, wikis, and social media posts are all becoming more common forms of assessment. The writing style may be more informal, in the first person, and therefore very different to the traditional academic writing style you may now be used to. However, clear communication is still going to be key as you navigate these more novel assignments.

Reflective writing, blogs, and social media posts are great for developing your communication skills and have real world applications too, since they may help you develop skills that you will use even after you graduate. In all cases you need to be aware of the purpose of the writing, who your audience is, be able to integrate information from various sources, and propose solutions. Reflective writing, blogs, wikis and social media posts are each described below.

Reflective writing

There may be times when you are required to do some reflection as part of your course, perhaps to help you think about how you learn in order to help you develop, or it could be as part of your work experience or placement where you reflect on what went well and what you would change, as you prepare for a specific career.

Reflection is all about you and it is your opportunity to write about your lived experience. In fact in many ways it is like a conversation with yourself. And because it is all about you, it is perfectly acceptable to write using 'I' and 'we' as your personal pronouns rather than the third person style you may have used in your academic writing. However, don't forget you will be submitting this for marking, so ensure your writing is clear and you avoid slang words. Check the word count requirements for your reflective piece, as this will provide an indication of how much depth you need to go into and how many scenarios you need to describe and reflect on.

But reflection is not just a description of a situation, it also includes analysis and evaluation. If you are not sure where to start, the 3 what questions can help you get going. The 3 what questions were originally defined by Rolfe, Freshwater and Jasper (2001) and consist of the following questions:

What? So what? and Now what?

The 3 what questions are further explained in Table 12.1.

Table 12.1 Three key questions for writing reflections

Key question	Explanation
What?	What is the situation, what occurred, what was my role?
So what?	What can I learn from this, what could I do differently, what are the broader issues or applications?
Now what?	What are the consequences, what do I need to do now, how can this be resolved or used to improve my practice?

Alternatively, if you wanted to take a more stepwise approach you could start with a **description** of the situation and how you felt, including your emotional response if appropriate too. Then try to **interpret** the experience, analyse what it meant. Follow this with an **evaluation**: how did this make you feel and how useful was the experience? Finally, create an **action plan** where you consider what you will learn from this and how you can plan to progress your learning further in the future. This approach is illustrated in Figure 12.1.

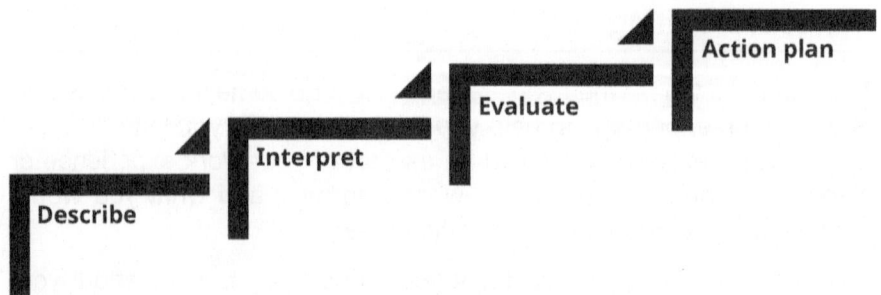

Figure 12.1 A stepwise plan for reflective writing

Compare the two reflective writing pieces in Box 12.1, both written by a student following a teaching placement. Which one is the most descriptive, and which one shows the most reflection?

Box 12.1   Examples of reflective writing

Writing excerpt 1

Today I observed a reception class. The class teacher came into the room and greeted the children and helped ensure they all put their coats on the right pegs. The first activity was the register, and the teacher waited until all the children were settled and quiet before she began. Then the children moved to different activities: a phonics table, card crafting or outside play. I was on the phonics table and the sound for today was the 'ch' sound. The session ended when the bell went for lunch.

Writing excerpt 2

On Wednesday 5 November I observed a reception class. The class teacher came into the room and was confident and warm as she greeted the children. She helped ensure they all put their coats on the right pegs, but she didn't do this for them, instead she gave clear instructions which the children followed. She waited for all the children to be settled and in their seats before she took the register, and the first activity began. The children were separated into groups based on ability and rotated different activities throughout the morning. The key activity was phonics and in particular the 'ch' sound, which the children were introduced to and practised. They were then asked to think of their own 'ch' words such as 'cheese', 'chips', 'chin' and 'chair'.

Throughout the lesson the teacher maintained an air of calm confidence which the children found reassuring and responded to. They were confident enough to join in and answer questions and give examples of their own. Similar to the findings of Gunning (2022) it is clear that Early Years teaching requires a distinct skill set that may be different to that required by teachers of older primary school classes, to help instil confidence in the children and ensure a sense of belonging in the class and the school. After observing this I realised I need to develop my own self-efficacy and talk to more experienced teachers in order to develop my confidence in the Early Years classroom.

Clearly, the first excerpt in Box 12.1 is descriptive but it also lacks detail and any form of insight. Whereas the second excerpt is not just longer, it is obviously more detailed, shows greater interpretation and analysis, but also considers what next in terms of personal development.

If your reflective writing piece does refer to a work placement and involves you mentioning work colleagues or patients, do protect their anonymity, make sure you don't use their names, or give away any information that could be used to identify them, and never be judgemental.

The whole idea of a reflective piece is to gain some personal insight to help you identify and report on the things that went well, and to help you process what may not have gone so well in order to learn from it (Health & Care Professions Council, 2021). Ultimately reflection is there to help you identify ways to improve your practice and enhance your own development.

Blogs

A blog is an online piece of writing. In the past a blogs were considered to be like an online journal or diary, but these days they are more like magazine articles. Anybody can create a blog, and they are certainly popular amongst social media influencers, but equally lots of lecturers have their own blogs and use them as a way of communicating to a wider audience about the research that they do.

If you wanted to write your own blog you would need to create a website or a sign up to a site that could host it, some of which are free e.g. Wix, Blogger and LinkedIn, etc. However, if you are writing a blog for a coursework assessment you will probably be asked to upload it to the university's virtual learning environment (VLE) e.g. Moodle, Blackboard, etc.

You might be asked to write a single blog post, however some assessments could be based on a series of blog posts that you write at different points during the term to reflect on the development of your learning.

You should approach a blog like you would a magazine article, so you want an attention grabbing title, definitely something that would attract clicks. You will need to stay focused on the topic and write in a concise manner because the average blog post is usually between 500 and 1,500 words – but check the word count you have been given if you are writing your blogs for an assessment. The other good thing about blogs is that because they are online you can put in links to websites and videos that you couldn't do in an essay.

Blogs are a great way to develop your own writing style. In many cases you can choose your own topics, develop your own original ideas, and write in a slightly less formal style. At the same time it is a great opportunity to learn to communicate with a wider audience through writing.

Wikis

You could be asked to contribute to a wiki as part of an assessment. A wiki is a bit like a website, but is usually less structured. You could describe it as being like a blog except it is more collaborative, and multiple users can edit the blog and interact on a single working document, so it is good for team projects. Wikis can be great for brainstorming and sharing information, whilst working on a common goal. With this sort of work, where you are all working on a common document, you do need to be respectful of what other students have written and ensure you value each other's opinions and additions, and don't erase them or change them just because it is not exactly as you would do it; allow everybody to contribute.

The most well-known wiki is obviously Wikipedia and anyone can edit this, but it is for this reason that it is not always the most reliable source of information, and therefore not so good to reference in your essays or reports.

Social media posts

Social media is a way of sharing information online in different communities and networks. Some of the most popular social media platforms include Instagram, X, Facebook, YouTube, WhatsApp, Pinterest, Slack, Snapchat, Strava, LinkedIn, etc. You may choose to be on some of these platforms for social reasons, but you could also be asked to engage with social media for an assessment. For example, if you were asked to create a marketing or a public health awareness campaign you might use social media to communicate your message widely. Whether the campaign goes live or is just a mock-up will depend on your university and the assessment, so find out as much information as you can about what you are being asked to do.

Social media posts are usually short and concise (with X, for example, there is a 280 character limit – see an example in Figure 12.2). However, where word limits are restricted you can always provide links to websites or blogs where more information can be provided. Photos and images are great to include as they can be really eye-catching, but think about the photo and its appropriateness, and has everybody in the photo given permission for the photo to be used? Alternatively you might even be asked to create a video for a platform such as YouTube.

Post

 Fruit and vegetables are an important part of a healthy diet. According to the Harvard School of Public Health they can help lower blood pressure and reduce the risk of heart disease 🥦 #5ADay

Figure 12.2 Example of a social media post on X for a public health campaign assignment

With this sort of assessment, you might not just be asked to create your own social media post, you may also be asked to look at and provide feedback on posts created by other students. If this is the case, be kind and try to ensure your comments are constructive.

With all forms of social media – think before you post! If you are posting on any social media platforms, don't forget they are public and can be seen by anybody including potential future employers. Therefore you may want to change your settings to make your account private in order to limit who can view your posts. Also, for personal safety you should check the geo-locator settings on all of your accounts.

Social media is not always the nicest place to be and you may come across aggressive people or trolls. Feel free to block them, or if you don't want them to know you have blocked them you can mute them. Consider taking regular breaks from social media and think about why you want to be on these platforms. Any harmful material or harassment (and you can use screenshots as evidence), should be reported to the police who should be able to offer further guidance.

> ## Top tip from a student 12.1
>
> *Consider setting your social media accounts to private and check your old posts, as future employers could look at your social media activity.* Jules

Chapter summary

Reflective writing, blogs, wikis and social media are all novel methods of assessment that you may come across at university. They are considered authentic assessments, meaning they are relevant to the world outside of academia and can offer a chance to develop some different employability skills. The writing style may be less formal, but that doesn't mean that there is less analysis or evaluation, in fact to the contrary, it is the evaluation that will provide the original insights. Whether you are writing a reflective piece, a blog, contributing to a wiki, or creating social media posts, consider your audience and aim for clear communication.

Check list

- If writing reflectively, make sure you don't just describe, but interpret, analyse and come up with an action plan
- A blog could be a great way to showcase your writing on a topic you are passionate about
- Wikis are great for team work and brainstorming, but do respect each other's contributions
- Remember social media posts are there forever, so think before you post

Further reading

Edwards, J. (2022) *Write Reflectively.* London: Sage.

13

Writing in Exams

Introduction

Nearly all university courses will include some exams, and understandably they can be a source of stress for many students. Exams are one way of encouraging students to engage with learning materials and module content and are a way of assessing both depth and breadth of knowledge. Rather than thinking of them with dread, try to see them as an opportunity to show what you know, and try to frame them in a positive light. With some solid preparation that includes active revision, exam practice, and a healthy perspective, you can ensure you will be ready to perform your best no matter what type of exam you are presented with, and produce your best writing in exam conditions.

Revision

Revision is key to doing well in exams. Ensuring you feel confident when you walk into the exam room, knowing you have done as much as you can, takes some preparation. Arguably it's never too soon to start revising, and as a minimum you should be reviewing your notes and other materials regularly, even weekly, to ensure that you can understand the notes you have made, making sure they are legible, and that you have all the information you need. This will save you time when you start your active revision.

Get organised

Firstly, you need to get organised. A revision timetable is a good idea so you can work out how much time you have to spend on each topic, allowing time for breaks and other activities that you need to do.

It's good to spread your studying out; you are more likely to retain more information if you do six hours of study spread across a week, rather than six hours in one go (remember 'chunking' from Chapter 1?).

You can organise your notes by date or, and probably more usefully, organise them by subjects and categories. You can use online folders, or colourful dividers for different subjects and then pull similar notes together.

Ensure you have all the notes

This might mean checking your lecture notes as well as the virtual learning environment (VLE) to ensure you have notes for every lecture and seminar, essay or report you have done as coursework, and checking the reading list for any recommended books or papers you were encouraged to read. Check your notes are complete and make an effort to fill in any gaps, using text books or even asking other students. You may also want to add more details to your notes and you can get that information from textbooks and journal papers.

Start condensing your notes

You will probably have a lot of material to revise, so you will want to start condensing this down. One way of doing this is to make notes from your notes, which encourages you to re-read all your materials whilst also writing down the most important parts; this in itself is active revision. You can then condense your notes down further by writing summaries of your notes. To help condense your notes you could consider writing bullet points, and using key phrases rather than full sentences; diagrams and flow charts can also be good. You can draw arrows and lines to connect information, underline words that could be used as headings, use highlighters to make important parts stand out, and use abbreviations to keep your materials concise. As you go through your revision notes, perhaps you can condense your notes down further to just one page, or even onto an index card.

Some studies have shown that making handwritten notes rather than typing can help you process information. Although typing can be quicker, Van der Weel and Van der Meer (2024) reported from a study of brain electrical activity that there were more elaborate brain connectivity patterns that promote learning when writing by hand, than when using a keyboard. Furthermore, if your exam is going to be written by hand with pen and paper there's certainly no harm in practising, as you might find you struggle to write for two solid hours if you are more used to typing than handwriting.

Check out past papers

It is important to know what style of questions you will be asked and how long you will have to complete the exam, and the best way to do this is to look at past papers. Your lecturers may give out past papers, but you may also find them in your university library or on the library website. Once you find the past papers, take a look at the style of the questions being asked, the terminology used, and also how the marks are allocated. Then have a go at completing the papers. Exam practice is one of the best ways of doing active revision. It tests your knowledge but can also help with your exam technique as well as your time management skills. If you can, you could even try completing a past paper in exam conditions so you can get used to this type of environment. After you have completed a past paper, mark your practice exam, as this is how you will identify what you know and what you don't know, and hence the areas where you need to do more work. If your subject doesn't have any past papers, perhaps you could ask your lecturer if they could provide some example questions. If you run out of past papers and example questions, you can do the same ones again to see how you have progressed, or even create your own. But overall, it cannot be emphasised enough how important it is to look at previous exam papers to see the sort of questions that can be asked, and to practise completing them in the allocated time frame.

Other revision tips you can try:

Writing model answers – this can be a good method if you have long questions or essay-based exams. If you don't have time to create a whole essay, detailed essay plans can be useful as well. Some programmes might even give you some exemplar answers, and it can be good to study these to see what makes a good answer. However, you need to be flexible and ensure you cover all the possible content from your course, because it is unlikely you will get the exact same question in your exam.

Flashcards – we mentioned condensing your notes earlier, and if possible condensing them down to fit on a flashcard. Alternatively, you can use flashcards to put a question or a key term on one side of the card, with the answer on the back, so you can test yourself or ask someone else to test you. Flashcards can be really handy to put in a pocket and carry around with you, so any time you find yourself with a few minutes to spare, such as while waiting for a bus, you can read over your flashcards (just remember to remove them from your pocket before you go into the exam room). Even the act of making your flashcards is a form of active revision, because you are learning the materials as you write them down.

Post-it notes – like flash cards, Post-it notes are a great way of condensing information, but with Post-its you can stick them anywhere, such as on your wall or mirror, so you keep seeing them and they regularly jog your memory and promote recall. You can also use them as book marks, or to write notes on particular pages (better than writing on the book itself), or even to plan an essay or create your revision timetable, as you can move the post-it notes around as much as you need.

Testing yourself or getting someone else to test you – you can use flashcards as outlined above, or cover your notes and test yourself, you might be able to find an online quiz, or just ask a friend to ask you questions from your notes.

Illustrating your notes – if you are a creative person you might find illustrating your notes and adding in diagrams useful. Drawing activates your visual memory which can help with the recall of information, so illustrate your notes and display them on the wall where you can see them.

Recording and listening to your notes – to make a change from reading, you could record your notes and then listen to them back whilst you are doing other things such as commuting.

YouTube – with so many videos available there are bound to be some that relate directly to the subject you are studying. However, be careful of the quality of the information, and ensure you don't just watch them passively; write notes or do the calculations as you watch to get the most out of them.

Blurting – this is a technique that was made popular by a YouTuber known as UnJaded Jade (2018). Essentially, it is where you write down everything you know about a particular topic. It's a good idea to set yourself a time limit, this might only be three minutes, but in that time you write down everything you can think of to do with that topic. Then the next part is key, this is where you check what you have written down by cross referencing it with your textbook or notes. Check the information is correct, make corrections and note down anything you left out. It's a good idea to do your checking in a different coloured pen, this way you can highlight what you don't know, as well as acknowledging how much you do remember.

Creating a study group – together you can check you have all the correct notes, explain to each other key concepts, and test each other on the course materials.

Removing all distractions – turn off the television and your phone to help retain your focus, then when you have done some revision you can reward yourself with some scrolling or by watching something on a screen.

Types of exams

There are many different types of exams, and therefore it is important you know which sort of exam you will be sitting so you can prepare appropriately. Terminology around exams and tests can vary, so make sure you know if your exam will be in person, or online, completed with pen and paper, or if you will be in a computer room. You might even be given an open book exam, and this might mean that you do the exam at home on your own computer, or it could even mean you can take notes into the exam. If you are not sure about the format of your exam then you should check with your lecturer.

The exams themselves can be organised and laid out in many different ways, so as mentioned previously it is important to look at past papers. The exam paper might include multiple choice questions, short answer questions that only require a couple of words or a sentence, long answer questions that could require at least a page or even an essay; your exam might even include a combination of these question types. But find out what sort of questions you are likely to get in advance so you can prepare for them accordingly.

Multiple choice questions (MCQ)

Multiple choice exams can be done online, or they could be completed on paper where you write the letter you think is the correct answer, or you circle the letter you think is the correct answer. You may even be given a special answer sheet where you shade a box to represent your answer e.g.:

Q1. a. ☐   b. ☐   c. ☐   d. ■

If you change your mind about an answer, make sure you put a clear X through the wrong answer and shade in the correct answer e.g.:

Q1. a. ☐   b. ■   c. ☐   d. ☒

Read the question carefully, in most cases there will only be one answer, but sometimes you may be asked to give more than one answer e.g.:

Q2. Which of the following are non-modifiable risk factors for osteoporosis:

  a.   *Age*
  b.   *Smoking*
  c.   *Gender*
  d.   *Alcohol consumption*
  e.   *Calcium intake*

This question would have two answers (a and c).

Check how much time you have to complete your MCQ as often the time allowed could be quite limited. Generally, when doing exams, it is a good idea to read the paper through from start to finish before you start to write down your answers, however with MCQ's, especially if time is short, you may want to get started straight away. If you get stuck on any questions it's best to move straight on to the next one, and then at the end come back to any questions that you haven't completed, when you how much time you have left. Once you have completed the exam, if there is still time left do go back and check your answers.

It is important to check how the MCQ will be scored. Often you will get one mark per question, however some MCQ's can include negative marking. Negative marking is where for every question you get wrong you lose a mark; this is to deter students from guessing answers they don't know. Not all universities use negative marking but it is worth checking so you know that if you are not sure of an answer whether it is worth attempting and guessing, or better to leave blank.

Short answer questions

These will generally test your knowledge and in some cases the application of knowledge. Generally, you should answer these questions in a concise and succinct manner.

Do check how many marks will be awarded for each question, as this can be an indication of how much you should write. A one-mark answer may just require one word, a phrase or sentence, but if a question is worth ten marks, then you would want to write considerably more.

If you don't understand the question, try deconstructing it or putting it in your own words; this can help you break down what is being required. Think about whether there are any key words you want to ensure you get into your answer, for example it would be very easy to describe the concept of sustainability without actually writing the word 'sustainability', yet the marks would be awarded for mentioning this key concept, so do make sure your answers include the technical terms and phrases relevant to your subject area.

If you don't know the answer, can you take an educated guess? It's always worth writing something as you could pick up some marks for writing some relevant information.

Long answer questions and essays

Read the exam question carefully and ensure you fully understand what is being asked. With long essay type questions it can really be worth spending a bit of time at the beginning of the exam writing out a brief plan. This plan won't be as detailed as a plan you might complete for a coursework essay, but it can be an excellent way of getting your thoughts in order and ensuring you don't forget anything. Your plan could be a list of the key things you want to cover, paragraph headings, or a quick spider diagram that maps out your answer.

Just like a coursework essay would have a structure, try to create a similar structure for your long exam questions. As a minimum your answer should have the following:

Introduction

Middle

Conclusion

The introduction should relate directly to the question and lay out what your answer will cover. The middle might include several paragraphs, and feel free to use paragraph headings if you think this will help you organise your answer. The conclusion should bring all your points together in order to answer the original question.

It is important you answer the question given, rather than just everything you know about a subject, so try to stay focused on the question. However, it is also important to write something, so if you are struggling to know what to write, go back to your essay plan and try to think of some key words as this might prompt you to remember other points you want to mention, and then once you get started other ideas will start to flow.

In exam conditions you won't be expected to memorise lots of references and produce a reference list. However, if you can, you should try to include some key references, as this can be a good way of showing what reading you have done. In this case the author and year will usually suffice e.g. (Olusoga, 2022).

Do keep going back to the exam paper and re-reading it to ensure your essay answers the original question that was given and hasn't gone off at a tangent. And do allow time at the end to read through your work and make any corrections or add any final points.

Plan your time

No matter what sort of exam you are sitting always plan your time well. If you have a two-hour exam and there are four long answer questions it would be obvious you should spend 30 minutes on each question. However, if you have an exam that is a combination of short and long answer questions you may want to divide your time up according to how many marks are at stake. E.g. if your exam is two hours and you know that 40% of the marks will be for short answers and 60% for two long answers you might divide your time as follows:

5 mins at the start for reading the paper

40 mins for short answers

60 mins for the two long answers (thirty mins each)

15 mins at the end for checking over your answers

Even if you think you have written everything you can, never leave an exam early. You never know if something might occur to you in the last five minutes. Spend your time checking your answers and correcting any spelling or grammatical errors.

Exam stress

Whilst exams may be a potential source of stress it is important to keep them in perspective, since stress is a normal response to something that can be challenging such as an exam. However, it can depend on your mindset as to whether this stress is a good thing or a bad thing. As part of a psychological research study, it was found that students who see stress as an opportunity for growth had less emotional exhaustion and generally performed better in their exams. Students that saw stress as a threat exhibited less effort and consequently delivered a poorer performance, highlighting that it is all about how you respond to stress (Shean, 2019). However, if you are suffering from high levels of stress or anxiety then you must talk to someone such as your university health and wellbeing advisor or your GP.

There are lots of things that you can do to reduce the stress around exams and some of these are listed below.

- Leave adequate time for revision. If you know you have put the work in, you can go into the exam room knowing you have done everything you can to put yourself in the best position to succeed
- Complete practice exams and if you can do them in exam conditions even better. John Hopkins University (2024) recommends what they term 'exposure therapy' with the aim of reducing stress around exams by mimicking those exam conditions when studying, so that they are more familiar to you

- If you find talking about exams increases your stress levels, then try to avoid talking to other students just before the exam
- Have a plan for what to do if you get into the exam room and your mind goes blank. For example, could you move onto another question, or write down some key words? This might also make you think of other ideas and then help you get a plan or a mind map onto paper
- Also have a plan for what to do if you feel anxious in the exam room. For example, this might be taking some deep breaths in and out, perhaps even closing your eyes and observing your breath for a few moments. Or distracting yourself by focusing on something else intently, like the grain of the wooden desk, or something outside the window. Then when you are ready, take another look at the exam question and start writing down some key words. The act of writing can be calming and will help direct your focus. Sometimes taking a few minutes to relax and stay calm will be time well spent and will help you get your focus back onto your exam
- After the exam, use the experience to work out what you could do differently next time you have an exam. Do you need some relaxation techniques, or do you need to get better at planning your time? Speak to your lecturer or health and wellbeing advisor about how best to approach your exams. If you have other exams, it's important you put this one behind you in order to focus effectively on the next one
- Try not catastrophize, you may have done better than you thought, and if nothing else you will have learnt from the experience, and this can help you prepare for next time
- Do take good care of your health and wellbeing (see Chapter 7 for more ideas). Make sure you get plenty of sleep, eat healthily, and try to exercise. Any is be good, but yoga or meditation can be particularly calming and helpful
- Speak to someone: make an appointment with your tutor, university health and wellbeing advisor or your GP

Specific learning differences

Students with specific learning differences may have been issued a Summary of Adjustments (SoA), sometimes called a Summary of Reasonable Adjustments (SoRA). These are documents that detail any adjustments that are deemed necessary so that you can demonstrate your academic abilities, ensuring fair and inclusive practice, providing access to appropriate support, and the removal of any potential barriers to your learning. If you have any form of disability or specific learning difference that could impact your studies you should arrange a meeting with your university's disability and/or neurodiversity office as soon as you can, even before you start your course, to find out what support is available. Depending on the details of your SoA, there may be specific arrangements to support you with exams, such as extra time to complete the exam, an ergonomic chair, use of a computer and keyboard, the exam paper could be written in braille or large print, you might be assigned a reader or a scribe, or given additional rest breaks, or have a separate room, or in some cases an alternative form of assessment. These arrangements will be specific to the individual but will take time to put in place, so please ensure you contact the relevant university office as soon as you can.

On the day of your exam

It's good to have a routine that you can follow. This could be waking up and starting the day with a healthy breakfast. Checking your bag to ensure you have your student identity card, a bottle of water, your pencils, pens and rulers in a clear pencil case or bag, and a calculator if you are permitted to use one.

Double check the time of the exam and in which room you will be doing it; sometimes locations change and if you are on a large campus, you will want plenty of time to get to the right place. Do make sure you leave early enough, allowing plenty of travel time, since traffic and public transport can be unpredictable, and you don't want to be rushing.

But most importantly try to stay calm and relaxed.

Top tip from a student 13.1

Always give yourself enough time to revise – leaving it to the last minute and cramming is just too stressful. Aida

---

Chapter summary

Everybody wants to perform their best on exam day and the best way to achieve this is through solid preparation. Organising and condensing your notes is a good place to start, and there are lots of ideas for different types of active revision to ensure you stay focused and productive. Past papers will also test your knowledge and familiarise you with the type of exam you will be sitting. But it is important to look after yourself during this time and ask for help and support when you need it.

Check list

- Don't leave your revision to the last minute
- Ensure you have a complete set of notes
- Condense and summarise your notes
- Find and complete some past papers
- Take good care of your physical and mental health
- Ask for support when you need it

Further reading

NHS (2023) Tips on preparing for exams. www.nhs.uk/mental-health/children-and-young-adults/help-for-teenagers-young-adults-and-students/tips-on-preparing-for-exams/.

14

Reviewing your Feedback So Far

Introduction

Feedback is an essential way of finding out how you are doing, what you are doing well and what you need to work on. It's not a personal criticism but a way of communicating information that is designed to help you gain confidence and improve your next pieces of work. This chapter will help you understand your feedback in order to make the most of it, and gain a greater understanding of the importance of feedback to improve the learning experience and inspire you to do even better in the future.

What is feedback?

The Centre for Teaching and Learning at the University of Oxford (2024) state that feedback is: 'information about a student's learning or performance which they can use in future work.'

This emphasises that feedback is not just a mark or criticism of your work, it is an important tool that you can utilise to develop your learning and improve on your upcoming assessments.

Feedback could be the written comments on an essay or report, the percentage mark for a multiple choice test, but it could also be an email, or verbal communication from your lecturer in a tutorial, it could even be from other students; feedback can be given in many ways and in all cases it is there to help you improve.

Students often focus on the score or percentage mark that they get for assessments, and pay little attention to the written or verbal feedback that they receive. But it is the comments that actually provide the most important cues and ideas based on what you have written and submitted. So it is important you read and understand the feedback in order to make the most of it and improve your next pieces of work.

Different types of feedback

As mentioned above, feedback can be given in many different ways and as such there are many different types of feedback. Feedback can be formal, such as on an essay that counts towards your overall degree, or it can be informal such as verbal feedback in the classroom. But there is also formative and summative feedback and these are described below.

In lectures you may be given some formative assessments to complete. These are activities where you can practise certain skills and get feedback, but the marks won't count. You can use the feedback from these formative assessments to improve any summative assessments.

Summative assessments are those where the marks do count – you will still get feedback and you should use this feedback to help improve your next pieces of work.

It is very easy to skip any formative assessments when you know the marks don't count and you have lots of other things you need to do. But you would be missing an opportunity to find out how you are doing, and get direct advice on how to improve your work and marks. Furthermore, you may receive formative feedback in lots of different ways, not just on written work; you can get formative feedback from class discussions, asking the lecturers questions, or feedback on draft documents. Be receptive to formative feedback and use it to increase your confidence and improve your summative work where the marks will count.

Your feedback might even occasionally be framed as 'feedforward'. Feedforward is essentially information that you receive that can provide guidance on how to do even better next time, and as such offers suggestions for improvements that are focused on future assessments.

Understanding grades and using marking criteria

Grades at university may be slightly different from the scales that you used at school. At school you might expect to get 100% on an assessment, whereas at university in the UK, anything above 70% is considered first class, though marks can still be awarded up to 100%. Table 14.1

helps explain the grading system for undergraduate degrees, where the pass mark is 40%.

Table 14.1 Understanding university grades

Degree classification	Percentage marks	Alphabetical ranking	Description
1st (first)	>70%	A	Excellent
2:1 (upper second)	60–69%	B	Very good
2:2 (lower second)	50–59%	C	Good
3rd (third)	40–49%	D	Pass
Fail	<40%	F	Fail

Some universities do have what they call a condoned fail, or a marginal fail: this where the mark is between 30–39%, whereas below 30% would be termed a clear fail. But this may come with further regulatory guidelines; for example, you may only be permitted to have one module that is in the condonable range. However, this can vary depending on the university, or if you are on an accredited course, so it is worth discussing with your tutor if you are at all worried about what this means.

Pass marks for postgraduate study are also slightly different, as the percentage needed for a pass at Master's level in the UK is 50%. There may also be additional classifications such as Merit where the final averaged mark is above 60% and Distinction if the mark is over 70%.

Most assessments you are given will also have a marking scheme that will explain how marks are awarded, and clearly describe the difference between work of different grades. These are similar to rubrics, though marking schemes may be slightly more detailed and more general, whereas rubrics are tailored for a particular assessment. Before you complete a piece of work you should study the marking scheme so you can see what the person marking your work is looking for. For example, you might be given marks for the following:

- Understanding
- Correct calculations
- Analysis
- Logical argument
- Presentation and correct word count
- Referencing

Marking schemes can vary, as can the percentage of marks given for each of the criteria that are listed, so look carefully at how the marks will be awarded.

After you have received feedback you should use the marking scheme again to make sure you understand how your mark was awarded. Once you understand how the marking schemes work, you can use them to mark your own work and develop your own feedback skills, to identify areas where you want to learn more, or where you may need to ask for some study skills support, and in doing so take control of your own learning journey.

Understanding feedback

It is important that you understand your feedback in order to learn from it. Most comments on your coursework should be should be self-explanatory, however there are some common remarks that regularly feature, and you might want to check that you fully understand their meaning; these are explained in Table 14.2.

Table 14.2 Common feedback remarks

Remark	Meaning
?	This probably means that the marker does not understand what you are trying to say; it could be the wording or it could be the argument. Try reading your work out loud to see if that helps identify what is not clear
Elaboration needed	More detail is required to explain your argument in full; add some study details if you can
Too descriptive	You may be doing too much describing and not enough critique and analysis. Can you show your understanding, identify limitations, show reasoning and evaluate the information?
More critical analysis needed	Similar to the point above, instead of just describing what you have read you need to critique it and put it in context, perhaps compare and contrast other views, and consider the strengths, weaknesses and applications
Could you clarify your point?	What you have written is not clear. It could be the sentence structure or it could be confusing. Think about the point you are trying to make, and use shorter sentences
This needs developing	This might mean that you are on the right lines, but you need to provide a bit more information or evidence. Perhaps an additional example would help, or more detail to explain how you arrived at your conclusion

Remark	Meaning
Writing not scientific/ academic enough	This could mean that your writing style is not very formal, perhaps it is a bit chatty or like a magazine article. Adding evidence, critique, and references will also add to the general scientific/academic style of writing
Relevance?	Have you gone off topic and lost your focus? Go back to your title or aim, and ensure all the information presented is relevant. Or perhaps you need a clearer explanation as to why your point is relevant
Bit unorganised	This might mean that your essay lacks structure; doing a plan before you start could help with this, and think about paragraph structure too. Or, if you are writing a formal report, have you got the correct information in the right sections (e.g. perhaps you have put some methodological details in the results section)?
No evidence of further reading	In most cases this relates to referencing, so ensure you refer to and reference everything you have read
Reference	You want to ensure that all your points are evidence based; reference where you get each piece of information. This comment means you are not using enough references
Write in your own words	This gives the impression that your writing is similar to another source, and therefore there is a risk of plagiarism. Alternatively if there is a change in your writing style this could indicate you have used AI. Always make sure you write everything in your own words to avoid these situations

In addition, it can also be useful to refer to the assessment guidelines and marking criteria that you were given when you started the assessment to understand how your work was marked. Did you follow the guidelines you were given, and as mentioned previously, how does your work compare to the marking criteria?

Most importantly, if you do not understand your feedback, you can ask your lecturer to explain it. Sometimes there is just a simple misunderstanding that can be resolved with a brief conversation.

Reflecting and learning from feedback: Kolb's Experiential Learning Cycle

It's important to read and reflect on your feedback so you know what you are doing right, and what you could improve upon. One way to do this is based on what is known as 'Experiential Learning Theory' (Kolb & Kolb, 2018). Experiential Learning Theory is well known in universities, and it is based on the idea that educationally you need to have the experience in order to learn from it, i.e. you can talk about an essay, but it is very hard to absorb and understand what it means to write an essay, until you have actually had a go at writing one, got feedback and learnt from it. The cycle also recognises that the learning doesn't happen in a straight line, it is a continual cycle of reflecting, thinking, and improving through trying.

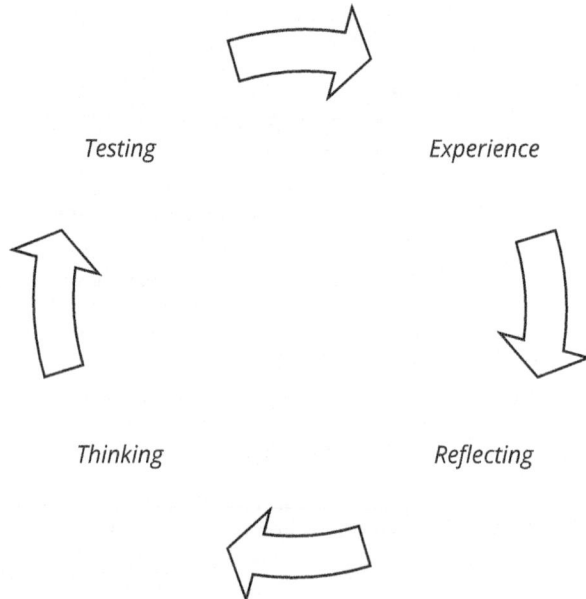

| Testing | Experience |
| Thinking | Reflecting |

Figure 14.1   Kolb's Experiential Learning Cycle (based on Kolb, 1984; Kolb & Kolb, 2018)

The four key areas of Kolb's Experiential Learning Cycle are:

1. **Experience** – this is the actual hands on experience – what was the experience or situation?
2. **Reflecting** – your reflections and observations to gain insight – what did you notice or feel?
3. **Thinking** – considering the theory – getting ideas and learning from your experience
4. **Testing** – putting your ideas into practice – in other words, trying out what you have learnt

You can use Kolb's cycle to reflect on your feedback. Table 14.3 gives an example of how you can use the cycle, in this case to reflect on an essay you submitted and got feedback from.

Table 14.3 Using Kolb's cycle to reflect on essay feedback

Point in the cycle	Practical example
Experience	Writing the essay and receiving feedback
Reflecting	How did you feel about the feedback, were the comments fair, were there things you could have done differently, did you leave it to the last minute, did you reference correctly?
Thinking	You think if you wrote an essay plan at the start this would have helped with your time management. You also realise you didn't reference correctly, so you ask a tutor or a friend for help with this and use the Cite Them Right website
Testing	Next time you write an essay, you start much earlier and create a plan, and you reference in the correct style, which you have now learnt to do

You can use Kolb's cycle for any type of assessment. The important thing is putting aside time to reflect and think about the work and the feedback in order to come up with a new plan that you can try out next time.

Receiving feedback

When you first get a piece of assessment returned to you after marking, you may be surprised by your own reaction. You might be really pleased with your mark, or you could even feel a bit disappointed. It is important to realise that these feelings are entirely normal, but please don't take them to heart – look at it as all part of the learning experience. Sometimes it helps to put the work away and come back to it a few days later; often when you come back to it, you'll realise the comments weren't as bad as you first thought. However, if you think the comments are unfair or don't make sense, then you should ask to speak to your lecturer. Sometimes it's easy to focus on the negative comments, but don't try to over-analyse them; they aren't personal, they should be seen as constructive criticism, with a view to helping you learn. But make sure you also make a note of the positive comments, as we often overlook these, and appreciate all the things you did well, and be proud of how far you have come.

Top tip from a student 14.1

I used to just look at the mark, but then I realised there was a lot more feedback and information on Turnitin than I first thought. Caleb

Chapter summary

Feedback is an important way of finding out how you are doing, high-lighting what you can do well, but also areas where you may need to develop particular learning skills. Use the marking criteria to really understand what the marker is looking for, and make the most of opportunities to ask questions and receive formative feedback in order to improve on your summative assessments. Read carefully the feedback you are given, and think and reflect on it, so you can use it to do even better on your next piece of work.

Check list

- Don't just look at the mark!
- Take your time to go through any feedback and ensure you fully understand it
- Make the most of opportunities for formative feedback
- Reflect on your feedback and think about how you might learn from it and do things differently next time
- If you don't understand the feedback, ask your lecturer or tutor

Further reading

Stone, D. and Heen, S. (2015) *Thanks for the Feedback: The Science and Art of Receiving Feedback*. London: Penguin.

Summary of Part 2

We have now considered the different types of written assessments and you will probably have submitted some of these assessments yourself. Do take the time to read any feedback that you receive as you can use it to further your knowledge and understanding of the work and to do even better in your next assignments. Now you have had a chance to put your writing skills into practice, and perfect the various types of written work you have been assigned, you are ready to embrace the next challenge – the dissertation.

THE DISSERTATION

Introduction to Part 3

Part 3 of this book, the final section, aims to guide you through all the stages of your dissertation from the planning and deciding on a research question, and developing an argument, to the writing of each separate chapter, from the abstract and introduction, the methods, results, discussion and conclusion, right through to the appendices. This part will also highlight differences that may be found in dissertations in different subject areas.

15

Getting Started on your Dissertation

Introduction

A dissertation is likely to be the largest piece of work you have ever written and this can be daunting. But with a bit of planning, and breaking the work down into manageable chunks, you can make the whole process a lot easier, and learn a lot of new skills along the way. This chapter will help you get started, by considering how to choose a dissertation topic, checking if you need to get ethical approval, developing your title, aims and research questions, whilst ensuring you keep the lines of communication open with your supervisor.

Dissertations

A dissertation may also be known as a thesis or a research project, but essentially it is a large piece of written work that includes some original research. The length of your dissertation may vary depending on your university, so it could be between 4,000 and 12,000 words, and is therefore likely to be the longest piece of work that you have completed to date. In most cases you will complete your dissertation during the final year of your degree, and you will certainly be spending a lot of time on it; for this reason it is important you find a topic that you really enjoy and want to study in depth.

Dissertations take many forms, depending on what programme you are studying. It could be qualitative or quantitative, it could be an audit, a survey, a systematic review, a meta-analysis or a narrative review, and if you are doing a science subject it may include some laboratory or field work.

Choosing a dissertation topic

In some subjects you may be able to choose your own dissertation topic. However, in other subject areas you may be given a list of possible options from which you need to choose a suitable topic. Therefore it is worth finding out how dissertation topics are decided at your university.

If you are given free reign, and you aren't quite sure what you want to research, then why not grab paper and pens and do a brainstorming session to try and narrow down your focus. You might like to consider some of the points listed below:

- Is your dissertation literature-based or will it involve some data collection?
- Do you prefer quantitative (numeric data) or qualitative (non-numeric data e.g. focus groups) methods?
- Do you like to do practical work in the laboratory or field?
- What topics interest you?
- What courses have you enjoyed the most?
- What books and articles have you recently read and enjoyed?
- Are there any areas of study that would be useful for your future career?
- Is there any emerging research or highly topical areas connected to your subject?
- Is there a member of staff that could supervise your chosen area?

Write down your answers and try to identify particular themes or key areas of interest to narrow down your ideas. Once you have narrowed down your focus to perhaps one or two ideas, it would be worth doing a brief literature search on each idea. This way you can see how much has been published on each topic. If one area has a lot of research that has been done previously this could be good in that it means you have a lot of work you can refer to, however it might mean that your dissertation idea is not that original. On the other hand, if there is very little published on your topic, this can show it is a unique idea, but it might make writing the literature review much more challenging.

You also want to ensure that the final project you decide on is something you are enthusiastic about and want to learn more about. Given that you could be spending quite a lot of time on your dissertation it is essential that it is something you will enjoy and not dread.

Finally you should discuss your ideas with your supervisor to check that your ideas are feasible and will be able to generate original research of the right depth.

Working with a supervisor

When it comes to a dissertation you should be taking the lead on the work and particularly the writing, however you will be allocated a supervisor and it is important that you communicate with them and meet regularly. In many cases you will be assigned a supervisor, but at some universities you may be given a list of projects that each supervisor can cover, and you can choose according to your interests.

Regular meetings are essential and it is important that you prepare for these. To begin with you should do some reading around the project and think about any questions you would like to ask. In later meetings you may want to bring drafts of any chapters you have written to get feedback on; in fact even better if you could email your chapters in advance of the meeting so your supervisor can read them and then give you feedback on your drafts in the meeting. However, if you don't have time to do any preparation you should still attend the meeting and use this as an opportunity to talk to your supervisor, explain your situation and get advice to help get back on track; cancelling or not attending is only likely to cause more problems further down the road.

The amount of feedback you can receive on drafts may vary; some universities allow the supervisors to look at every chapter once, some may look at multiple drafts, some will only look at one chapter, in which case make sure it is the chapter that you find the most challenging, perhaps the results chapter or the discussion and interpretation of the results. But do use the opportunity to submit work and receive feedback as this can only improve your writing.

It's good to take notes during your supervisory meetings, as it is easy to forget some of the details, and some universities may even require you to keep a record or a log of your meetings; this could be particularly important for evidence, if you later feel that you weren't given enough supervision or you found it difficult to get hold of your supervisor. If this is the case you should speak to your programme leader sooner rather than later. Although rare, it is possible that you may clash with your supervisor or simply do not get on. In such cases make sure you are always professional and respond to emails promptly and show up to meetings, perhaps you just need to have a conversation to address your concerns or to align your differing expectations; aim for a negotiation rather than a confrontation (Adrian-Taylor et al., 2007). Having meetings with other students who are doing similar projects may also help change the dynamic. However, if your concerns are more serious then you should speak to the module or programme leader, or even the Head of Department immediately.

Aims

It is important your research has a clear aim. An aim puts in writing the purpose of your study and what you hope your research will achieve. The aim can be relatively broad and it is usually only one sentence (or at the very most a short paragraph), such as in the examples below:

a.   The aim of this study is to investigate the nutritional knowledge of ballet dancers
b.   This paper aims to explore how themes of identity are configured in Shakespeare's sonnets
c.   The aim is to evaluate the sustainability of global supply chains

Whilst the aim can be quite general, the aim is often followed by research objectives or research questions, which are much more specific.

Research objectives

Research objectives will set out what exactly you need to do to achieve your aims, and they should relate to the purpose of the project and the approach you will take. This can break down the research into smaller achievable sections, and so you may have several objectives (often between two and five); think of them as the stepping stones that will help you achieve your aims.

For example, if your aim was to:

Investigate adherence to a gluten-free diet in people living with Coeliac disease

You objectives might be:

1.   Explore the literature on adherence to a gluten-free diet
2.   Understand the methodological challenges of assessing adherence to a gluten-free diet
3.   Identify the barriers to adhering to a gluten-free diet in people living with Coeliac disease

Think about what you need your objectives to be in order to achieve your aim. You can use the words below as prompts:

- Explore
- Gain understanding
- Investigate
- Review

- Test the theory
- Evaluate
- Analyse
- Compare

Make sure each objective is clear and distinct, and that they don't overlap each other. If you achieve each of the research objectives that you have set out, then you should automatically be able to achieve your research aim.

Research questions

Like research objectives, research questions need to be very specific, and they are essentially the questions that you set out to answer in the course of your dissertation.

Some examples of research questions are given below:

a. Do first year students that attend programme induction perform better in problem-based learning assessments than non-attending students?
b. How does the portrayal of women in 1930's literature reflect American society in the pre-war years?
c. What is the effect of a vegan diet on the gut microbiota?
d. Do hospital night shift workers have lower levels of job satisfaction and stress than day shift workers?

To write your research question, consider What, How, Where, and Why:

- What are you investigating?
- How will you investigate this?
- Where will the study take place?
- Why is your study important?

Think about the questions listed above and then try to draft your research question. You can draft it, and then refine your question to make it more precise and concise.

If you are still having difficulties coming up with a research question, there are different frameworks that you can use. One that is commonly used in mixed methods research is known as SPIDER and was originally proposed by Cooke et al. (2012), as shown in Figure 15.1.

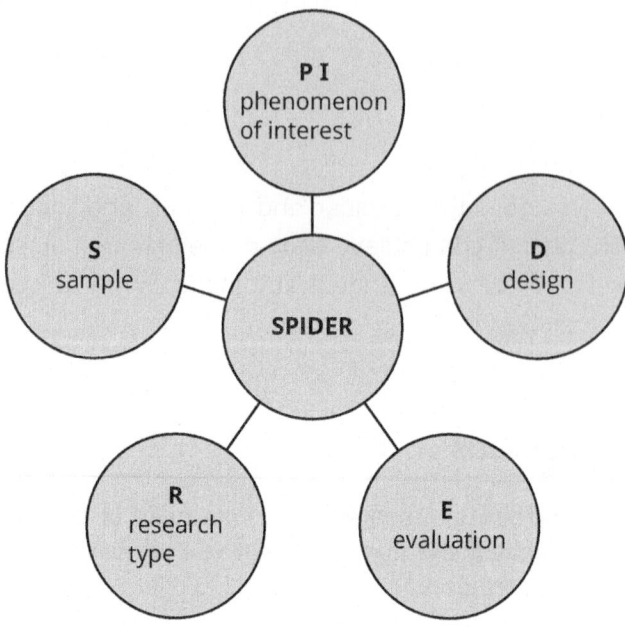

Figure 15.1 The SPIDER research framework

The SPIDER research framework can be explained as follows:

S = Sample – who are you studying? E.g. Nursing students

PI = Phenomenon of interest – what is the topic being investigated? E.g. experience of placements

D = Design – what technique and methods will be used? E.g. focus groups

E = Evaluation – what are the outcomes of the study? E.g. experiences

R = Research type – what sort of research are you doing? E.g. qualitative

Using the examples given above, a suitable research question could be:

What are the experiences of student nurses on clinical placement?

If the SPIDER research framework doesn't work for your project you might want to consider PICO instead (Richardson et al., 1995). PICO is often used for clinical or intervention type studies. PICO is explained below:

P = Patient, population or problem e.g. recreational runners

I = Intervention e.g. a sports drink

C = Comparison e.g. a placebo

O = Outcome e.g. levels of fatigue

Using the examples given above, a suitable research question could be:

Does a sports drink reduce fatigue in recreational runners?

It is a good idea to keep coming back to your research question throughout your dissertation to remind yourself of your original intentions and to ensure you stay on topic.

In some subject areas you will be asked to present your hypothesis; this could be in addition to the research question or instead of it. The hypothesis is your prediction of the outcome of your research, and you may use your literature review to help predict this. The research question and the hypothesis should certainly be complementary. For example, the research question and the hypothesis for a study looking at the effect of light availability on plant diversity in woodlands could be:

The research question: *Does light availability affect plant species diversity in English woodlands?*

The corresponding **hypothesis**: There will be richer plant species diversity in areas with greater light availability

You may have more than one research question and even several hypotheses depending on your project, however you should avoid having too many, as you want to be able to respond to them all, and no dissertation can cover everything.

You should set out your aims, objectives, research questions and your hypotheses before you start your study; however, you probably do not need to have all four. If setting out your aims, objectives, research questions and hypotheses would be too much, check your dissertation handbook to see if there is guidance or ask your supervisor if they have a preference.

Titles

Titles need be informative and self-explanatory (Levin, 2011). If you are not sure where to start, have a look at some journal articles in your subject area for ideas. The title should be as specific as possible, nothing too broad or vague. You should also avoid surplus words, for example phrases at the start of the title such as 'a study to investigate...' can probably be deleted without affecting the rest of the title. Consider the title below:

A study to investigate flexible work policies

You can remove the phrase 'a study to investigate' and it is still clear that the dissertation is about flexible work policies. However, this is not very specific, the title says nothing about where the study is based or if it is in a particular industry, or what specifically will be assessed in relation to flexible work policies, or the people that will be involved; that information all needs to be added. A much more specific title would be as follows:

Flexible work policies in the UK financial sector and the impact on work–life balance for new parents

At the same time, you don't want to make your title too long, as that could become confusing.

If your study is a literature-based study, such as a narrative review, a systematic review or a meta-analysis, you might want to specify that in the title. For example:

The history of reflexology as an alternative therapy: a narrative review

It's always good to have an attention grabbing title, but remember not everyone will have the same sense of humour as you. You can always use a colon to split the title into two parts if you want to have something a bit eye-catching, but at the same time also provide a bit more study detail e.g.:

Goldilocks' dilemma: optimum amounts of sugar and salt for the preservation of tinned vegetables

Should your dissertation change course, then you may want to change your title, and this is usually fine (unlike hypotheses which you should never change), but it is worth checking with your dissertation supervisor first.

Research proposal

Before you start your research you are likely to have to complete a research proposal to ensure the project is feasible and safe. What this entails may depend on the university, and this may be a short form that simply asks you to write down what your dissertation aims to achieve and how you will go about it. However, some universities may ask for a much more in-depth research proposal that could be presented as an ethical approval form (explained later in this chapter) and sometimes in addition to an ethics form.

A typical research proposal contains the following headings:

- **Project title** – this should be clear and concise and make clear what the project is about
- **Background** – introduce the area you wish to study, and some key literature in this area. You could also state why this research is needed or who or what it would benefit
- **Research question or aim** – what you are setting out to discover, ensuring this is something that you can test and answer
- **Study design and methods** – this section is key to your proposal, as it should describe exactly how you will go about your study. Is it quantitative or qualitative, experimental or a survey, will you be collecting original data or relying on primary and secondary sources? Where will the data be collected and using what method and with what equipment? You should also report how you propose to analyse the data
- **Ethics and risk assessment** – this will be a brief overview of the risk in the proposal, since if you are doing a project that involves humans, animals or any sort of risk you are likely to be required to complete a full ethics form and a health and safety risk assessment, both of which will contain much more detail, before you can start to collect any data (see the next section)
- **Conclusion** – summarise the overall proposal and clarify the purpose of your dissertation
- **References** – list all the references used to write the proposal

A research proposal is usually written in a very concise style, and makes clear what your research will contribute to the subject area.

Ethics

If you are doing a project that involves humans, animals or products including tissues and cells from humans and animals, or collects any sort of personal information, you must have ethical approval before you can start. Most scientific studies will require ethical approval, as will any type of survey that involves people. It is recommended that before you start any study you consider the ethical implications of your work. If you are doing a literature review-based dissertation then you will probably not need to complete an ethics form nor get ethical approval for your study. However, if you do need to get ethical approval, your supervisor should advise you on what you need to do. Most universities will have some standard forms that you will need to complete. If you are doing a study that involves any other organisation, e.g. the National Health Service (NHS), then you may also need to get ethical approval from them too.

An ethics form is an official document that requires you to consider the implications of your research, and according to the Economic and Social Research Council (2021) should typically include:

- The title and the aim of the research
- The names of all involved in the research, and details of any conflict of interests
- The study design and the methods for data collection and analysis
- Details about any participants including how many you aim to recruit, where you will recruit them from, and any inclusion or exclusion criteria. In particular you should be clear if this includes any person who could be considered vulnerable
- Any potential ethical issues that could arise and how these will be addressed
- How the data will be managed and kept secure, and mechanisms for data anonymisation and/or sharing
- Any risks to participants or third parties, and how this will be minimised and monitored
- Any benefits of the research to any participants or third parties
- Information about the study that will be given to participants, including informed consent
- Health and safety considerations (there may be additional forms for this)
- Potential risks to the researchers and how they will be supported and protected
- The impact of the study and how this will be communicated
- Start dates and duration of the study

Once you have submitted your ethical approval forms, you must wait until you receive official confirmation that your study has been approved before you start to collect any data.

There may be certain conditions with which you need to comply before you can get started, and so you should wait until you get the go-ahead from the ethics committee or your supervisor. It can be quite a time–consuming process to request and receive ethical approval, so ensure you factor this into your planning.

Informed consent

You may have noticed in the list above that informed consent is mentioned. This is an essential part of any study that involves human participants, as they need to be adequately informed about the study and freely give their consent in order to participate.

Please note we use the word 'participants' rather than 'subjects', as people should be able to freely participate in research rather than be subjected to it (Boynton, 1998).

Your university will probably have a standard template for a participant consent form, but a typical template will follow the outline shown in Box 15.1.

Box 15.1 Template for a participant consent form

Title:

Outline of the project:

Contact details for the lead researcher:

A statement of consent, for example: I give my informed consent to participate in this study. I understand that I am free to withdraw from the study at any point.

I understand that my data will be treated in strict confidence and stored in an anonymised form, and this may be published as part of aggregated results.

Signature ....

Name ....

Date ....

If you are concerned about anything at all please do contact the research supervisor, or if you would like to contact an independent person please contact the Head of Department.

Research Supervisor contact details:

Head of Department contact details:

Do make sure you are clear about what will happen to any data that is collected and how it will be kept safe e.g. a password protected computer, and the duration for which the data will be kept. You should also clarify what happens if a participant decides to withdraw from the study: can their data be withdrawn too? If the data is anonymised perhaps this would be impossible.

Confidentiality for participants is important, as is anonymity, and therefore you may need to give your participants an ID code to ensure this.

In such cases, you need to store any data or questionnaires separately from the consent forms, which will include the participants' names.

General Data Protection Regulation (GDPR) will also apply to your dissertation if you are collecting personal data, so you must ensure you abide by the seven principles laid out by the Information Commissioner's Office (ICO, 2024) which are as follows:

- Accountability
- Accuracy
- Integrity and security
- Limitations on the length of storage
- Minimisation of data
- Purpose limitation
- Transparency, fairness and lawfulness

Only collect the data you need for your study and be sure to keep it strictly confidential and secure. For more information check out the Information Commissioner's Office website: https://ico.org.uk/.

Health and safety risk assessments

A health and safety risk assessment is to protect anybody involved in your study, including you! The main aim is to identify any potential hazards, considering who could be affected and how, making an assessment of the risk, putting in control measures, monitoring the work, and keeping up-to-date records. Hazards could be anything from biological agents, fire risk, the weather, emotional distress or lone working, and so it is important that the person who completes the health and safety risk assessment has been trained how to do so. For this reason it is important that you talk to your supervisor and/or the technician team at your university to get advice.

If you have any questions about ethics, informed consent, data protection, and health and safety risk assessments, then you should speak to your supervisor or programme leader before starting your dissertation.

Planning your time

Find out the final submission date for your dissertation, and put that in your diary/planner in big red letters. But also check if there are any other deadlines associated with your dissertation. You may be given dates by when you should complete each chapter. In some cases these are soft deadlines that you can use as target dates in order to stay on track and complete in a timely fashion, but at some universities these may be hard deadlines that you need to stick to, so make sure you make a note of these dates and plan accordingly. You may also be required to give a presentation or attend a viva (please note not all universities do this) in which case make sure you get those dates and put them in your diary or planner too.

It is a good idea to map out when your deadlines are over the year – an example of this can be seen in Table 15.1.

Table 15.1 Dissertation deadlines

Month	Action
Oct	Agree dissertation topic with supervisor
Nov	Complete first draft of the introduction and literature review
Dec	Write the methodology and start data collection
Jan	Continue data collection and start data analysis
Feb	Write the results chapter
Mar	Complete the discussion chapter
Apr	Write the conclusions
May	Write abstract and general editing
	Hand in dissertation 21st May
	Dissertation viva 28th May

As well as mapping out your deadlines for the whole academic year, it is also a good idea to plan what you will do on a weekly or even daily basis too. You can break each chapter down and have smaller targets to complete; taking it step by step can also help the whole dissertation seem less daunting. Some students like using Post-it notes to plan what task they will do each day; you can stick these to your wall or desk and they are handy as you can move them around as needs be. If you need a reminder of how to be an effective planner, look back at Chapter 1 for ideas on how to create term, weekly and daily planners.

Top tip from a student 15.1

Never be afraid to reach out to your supervisor and admit you're feeling over-whelmed or struggling to manage the workload. Having someone explain things really makes it a lot more manageable – a problem shared actually is a problem halved! Jemma

Chapter summary

Getting started on your dissertation can be one of the hardest parts. But once you get going it will be clearer what you need to do next. Start by identifying your areas of interest, and then narrowing these down to find a particular area of study. Think about your title and ensure it conveys exactly what your dissertation is about, and set out your aims, objectives and hypotheses before you start your study. You must find out if you need to complete a research proposal, an ethics form, and health and safety risk assessment, as these must be completed before you collect any data. Plan your time well, and try to focus on one chapter at a time rather than the whole thesis in one go.

Check list

- Decide on a topic and set out your aims and objectives
- Think carefully about your title and your research question and hypothesis
- Find a suitable supervisor and arrange a tutorial meeting
- Before you get started check if you need to complete an ethics form or a health and safety form
- Make a planner to give yourself targets, and make a note of any deadlines particularly the final submission date

Further reading

Becker, L. (2015) *Writing Successful Reports and Dissertations*. London: Sage.

16

Writing your Introduction

Introduction

Now you have chosen your dissertation title, and set out your aims and hypotheses, you can start to write your introduction. The introduction will really set the scene for your dissertation and help the reader understand what your dissertation is all about, and what it will add to the existing knowledge in your field of study.

It should also be noted that instead of having an introduction chapter, followed by a literature review chapter, some universities recommend combining these into a single chapter. Whilst this chapter will focus on the introduction, and Chapter 17 will focus specifically on the literature review, both chapters will still be relevant to you, even if you are writing a combination chapter.

Organisation of the introduction and literature reviews

The main aim of the 'introduction' is to literally introduce your dissertation. However, as mentioned in the introductory paragraph, depending on your programme of study there might be slight differences in the way introduction and literature review chapters are organised. The possible structures for a typical dissertation are shown in Figure 16.1. Most dissertations will have an abstract and chapters for the methods, results, discussion and conclusion. However, when it comes to the introduction and literature reviews different universities and subject areas may prefer these presented in different ways. Some universities keep the introduction and literature reviews separate as two individual chapters, whereas some prefer you to have one chapter that covers both the introduction and the literature review together. Furthermore, you might even find that in some subject areas, such as English Literature, the literature review is interwoven throughout the whole dissertation rather than a single identifiable chapter (Ridley, 2012), and where this is the case you need to ensure you have a clear introduction chapter so you can set out your study, before you move onto the review of the literature.

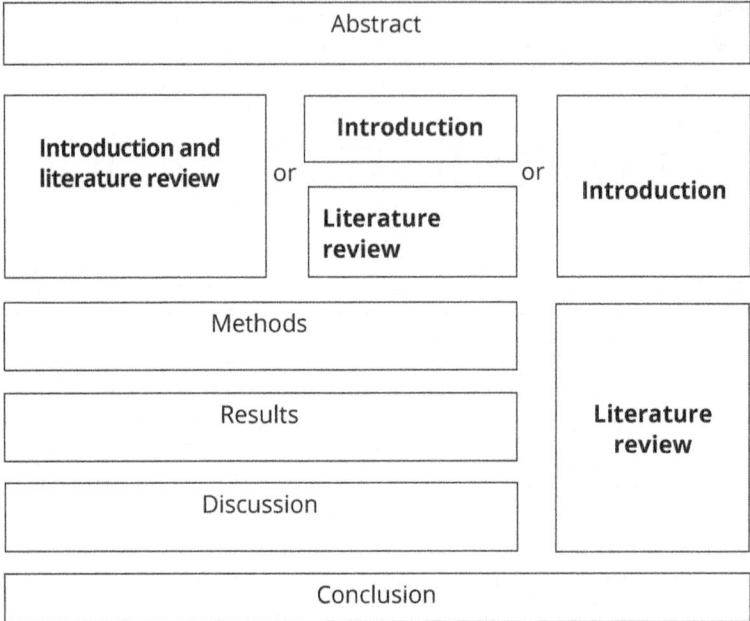

Figure 16.1 Possible structures of a dissertation

If you are required to write an introduction and a literature review as separate chapters, your introduction could be a few pages (often 5% of the total dissertation). However, if you are doing a combined chapter, the introduction may only be one or two paragraphs or a single page. The introduction does not need to be a long chapter, but it does need to set out a clear rationale for your study.

Structure of an introduction

All introductions need to cover the same elements, but those that are a complete chapter will go into more detail than those that are just the opening paragraphs to the literature review. Either way, all good introductions should explain the following:

- Why your chosen topic is interesting
- The focus of your research

- The value of your study
- Your aims and hypothesis

These are explained in detail below.

Why your chosen topic is interesting

You want to get the readers interested in your topic right from the very start and so you want your introduction to be the hook that draws your readers in, and entices them to want to read more. Presumably you found the topic interesting and that is why you chose to research it for your dissertation, so try to put into words what it is that fascinates you about the topic. The information in this section can be reasonably general, however don't start this too generally as you can assume your readers will have some knowledge in the area of study. For example, if your dissertation title is 'The chemistry of pesticides in agriculture' you don't need to explain what chemistry is, as you can assume the readers will have at least that level of understanding of the subject.

The focus of your research

It is important to clarify how you intend to approach your dissertation, perhaps even with a brief overview of your theoretical approach or your methodology, and what your dissertation will cover. In order to explain the focus of your research, you will need to briefly refer to the core literature in this area, this should include some background information and in particular any seminal or key papers. You do not have to go into great detail here, more of an overview, because the literature review will be your opportunity to explore the background in depth, but you should ensure that the key papers are referred to. At this point you may also need to describe the key concepts in your area of study, and define any specific terms that you will be using. Depending on the topic of your dissertation, you may also want to include some key statistics to further strengthen the case as to why your dissertation is needed.

The value of your study

What is your motivation for the research? More specifically, what will your research add to the field of study, and why is this significant? Perhaps your findings will refine a new method, help people understand a topic, offer a new insight, perhaps give hope to those living with illness, or extend knowledge, or fill a gap in the existing literature; you should highlight here whatever is new and novel about your dissertation.

Your aims and hypothesis

These were covered in the previous chapter, as they are important to set out before you start your dissertation so they are clear in your mind, plus you will need them when writing your research proposal and ethics forms. However, they should be clearly presented at the end of your introduction as well; you can also include your objectives here too.

At this point you may also want to give an indication of the structure of the dissertation that will follow, and an overview of what the subsequent chapters will cover e.g.:

'Chapter 2 will explore the literature in-depth in order to provide a deeper understanding of the need for further research in...'

'Chapter 3 describes the methodology used to....'

'Chapter 4 presents the results of...'

'Chapter 5 discusses the key findings and makes comparisons with previous studies in literature, and the thesis is concluded in Chapter 6.'

However, it should be noted that not all subject areas require students to include this overview of the chapters, so find out from your supervisor what is expected at your institution.

After reading your introduction chapter (or section), the reader should know exactly what you are researching, how you are going to do it, and why your research is needed.

Overall shape of the introduction

Sometimes it helps to visualise the shape of the introduction chapter. The introduction has often been described as following an inverted triangle or pyramid structure (Buczkowski, 2023a; Maier, 2013); see Figure 16.2.

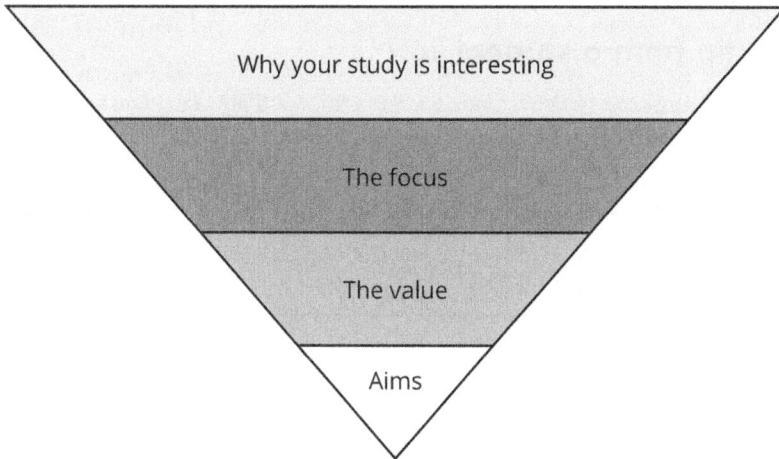

Figure 16.2 The inverted pyramid view of the introduction

At the top, the broadest part of the pyramid, is where you are stating why your chosen topic is interesting; this is the most general information, but also includes the 'hook', i.e. an interesting opener that will make the reader want to read more. Then as you move down the pyramid you start to become more specific and explain the focus of your study, this is followed by the value of your particular study, and finally at the narrowest point of the pyramid you present your aims and hypothesis.

Some students find it easier to work backwards, so if you already know what your aims and hypothesis are you already have your specific focus at the tip of the pyramid, then you can work backwards up the pyramid to find the broader context for your research.

When to write your introduction

Although the introduction is the first chapter in your dissertation, you do not have to write this first. Some people prefer to write their introduction much later on in the process, perhaps after data analysis, when they know exactly what it is they are introducing. However, an introduction can help you get your ideas together, set out the key concepts and therefore help with the planning, so you may want to get started on this chapter straight away. If you want to tweak it later on, once you have finished your other chapters, then that is fine too.

> ## Top tip from a student 16.1
>
> *I found it easier to write my introduction chapter after I had finished all the other chapters and when I was clear on the story I wanted my dissertation to tell.* Dean

Chapter summary

Introductions can be an individual chapter or combined with a literature review, and this may vary by university. But all introductions should include a description of why your chosen topic is interesting, the focus of your particular research, the value of your study, ending with your aims and hypothesis; visualise it as an inverted pyramid. The introduction does not have to be written first, instead write it when you are clear on the overall picture that your project is presenting.

Check list

- Find out if you need to do separate introduction and literature review chapters or a combined one
- Visualise the structure of your introduction as an inverted pyramid
- Consider what you find interesting about your topic and why you chose it
- What will your findings add to the field of research?
- Present your aims and hypothesis at the end of your introduction

Further reading

Levin, P. (2011) *Excellent Dissertations*. Maidenhead: McGraw Hill.

17

Completing the Literature Review

Introduction

Writing the literature review will give you the opportunity to put into practice all the academic writing, critical reviewing and referencing skills that you have developed so far.

In this chapter you will want to set the scene and explore in detail the previous research that has been conducted and that led to your study. By critiquing the studies that have preceded yours, you will be able to put your dissertation into context and highlight what your dissertation will bring to the subject area.

Overview of a literature review chapter

The literature review chapter is a detailed summary of all the research and studies that have been conducted in your area of research previously. Although it is a summary of the subject area you will need to ensure you provide the right level of breadth and depth, and critique the literature thoroughly in order to define and contextualise the research question that you want to answer. Like in the introduction, the literature may start relatively broad as you describe the subject area, but then you need to ensure you add further depth by presenting a detailed critique of specific and key papers relevant to your dissertation.

Literature reviews should always include all the most recent current research, but you may also want to provide some historical background or context depending on the topic of your dissertation, and there may be some classic papers or books that you want to include. The literature review will probably also include a review and critique of previous methodologies that you can also use to justify the methods that you will employ. Essentially, it is important to have a body of knowledge to which you can relate your own findings (Hart, 2018), as you will need to return to the themes that you raise in the literature review in the discussion chapter.

The key differences between a strong and a weak literature review are shown in Table 17.1.

Table 17.1 Differences between a strong or weak literature review

A strong literature review:	A weak literature review:
Is a critical review	Is mostly descriptive
Is a complete synthesis of existing research	Is a list or at best an annotated bibliography
Has the right levels of breadth and depth	Is too narrow and or too shallow
Makes clear how each paper is relevant to your study	Is unclear on the relevance of the papers you are reviewing
Is clear and concise	Is confusing

How to get started

1. Firstly, identify the key search terms that you will use to find papers relevant to your study. You could start by picking out key words from your title and hypotheses, think of similar words (synonyms), and also include both American and UK spellings. You can also see what key words authors of papers on similar studies have used, as many journal papers list key words under the abstract

2. Start by searching for literature, and reading around the subject. Perhaps your supervisor has recommended some papers, or you might start with Google Scholar but then look at databases specific to your subject (see Chapter 3 for more details). If you find a good paper, take a look at the reference list, as this can be a good way of finding other relevant papers

3. Make a note (online or on paper) of each paper you read, as you will want to come back to these later

4. Critique the papers: what were the key findings, and the strengths of the authors' approaches? But also, what could have been done differently, and how could the study have been improved?

5. Try to collate similar papers and make comparisons across studies. You could create a table to help with this and highlight where the papers agree and disagree

6. Try to consider how each paper is relevant to your research; it might be obvious to you, but you will need to make this clear for the reader

7. Once you have started grouping similar papers together, start to think about the structure of your chapter. Use the topic of each group of papers to help come up with paragraph headings (you can always change or remove these later)

8. Make a plan for the chapter, using the paragraph headings. Consider what is the theme of each paragraph, as you want each paragraph to offer a themed synthesis of the key findings

9. Think about how you will link from one paragraph to the next, starting broad and getting more specific as the chapter progresses

10. When you are happy with your plan, then you can start to add detail to each of the paragraphs, including the in depth critique of the papers, and the references

Structure of the literature review

Structures of literature reviews can vary. One of the most popular ways of organising the literature is to have a thematic structure, where the papers you review are grouped by theme. As described above in the section 'How to get started', this is where you group similar papers together; usually you would start with the broadest group themes first and then narrow down to the more specific publications.

However, you may wish to organise the structure of your literature review differently, and perhaps if you are writing about a topic that has evolved over time you may wish to organise your literature review according to chronological order, usually from the oldest publications to the newest resources.

Another approach would be to combine the thematic and chronological structures (University of Southampton Library, 2024). This is where you might group the papers you review into themes, but then within each theme present the information in chronological order.

Some dissertations cover two or more different areas of study, for example in a study of 'smoking and alcohol consumption in young adults', you might want to divide the literature review into a major section on smoking, a major section on alcohol consumption, and then a section where you consider levels of smoking and alcohol consumption in young adults in particular. Within each of these major sections you may want to organise the papers into sub themes, or put them in chronological order.

You can give each paragraph heading and subheading a number, and this can also help with the flow of the chapter for example:

2 The literature review

2.1 Background to the field of research

2.1.1 The origins of the research

2.1.2 How the field of study evolved

2.2. New developments

Structuring your literature review and numbering your paragraphs will help keep the chapter logical and organised.

Adding the details

Once you have refined the structure of your dissertation you will want to start adding the detail and ensuring you have enough depth. Your literature review should cover all the key concepts and current theories in your area of study, so even a reader with no knowledge of the subject will feel like they have a clear understanding of the research in this area. You will also want to highlight where there are gaps in the literature and where there are still unanswered questions, as it is these gaps where further research is needed and where your dissertation may be able to help fill the gap.

You will also want to highlight where there are disagreements or controversies in the literature. This can follow the usual format of an academic argument. An academic argument is where you present your particular take on a topic, and then debate the evidence for and against the point you are trying to make. Remember the stepwise structure of an academic argument (from Chapter 4):

- Make your point
- Present the evidence
- Offer the counter argument
- Summarise and draw conclusions

Try to ensure your argument is balanced and clear and that you evaluate the arguments that other authors have put forward (Cottrell, 2008). You may agree with some points and not others but try to present all view points, and use evidence to argue your point strongly. It may be that at this point there is no clear answer to the arguments put forward, so you may also want to highlight where any controversies still remain, and perhaps how your research will address this.

Theoretical frameworks

Not all undergraduate dissertations will have a theoretical framework; this very much depends on the subject you are studying, since they are more common in social sciences and at higher levels of study, but if you are required to provide a theoretical framework, the literature review chapter is usually the best place to put it. A theoretical framework is less about providing a rationale for the study, which your literature review should do anyway, and more about stating which approach or orientation your study will take, and providing a structure for the research being conducted to follow (Luft et al., 2022). As part of the theoretical framework you should highlight the key concepts and variables being studied and present their definitions, and any existing specific theories. These theories are important as they will inform the choice of methods you use to collect your data. The framework can also be used to limit the scope of the research by highlighting which variables the study will focus on (and which ones it won't) and therefore define the focus of the study and set the limitations. Theoretical frameworks are usually written in the present tense (Sacred Heart University Library, 2020). For more on theoretical frameworks see the book by Bingham, Mitchell and Carter (2024) in the Further Reading section at the end of this chapter.

Citing your sources

References are going to be key in a literature review, so make sure you make a note of all your sources and have another read of Chapter 5 if you need to brush up your referencing skills.

In the sciences, you will probably want to try and avoid direct quotes, saving these for rare occasions, however in arts-based subjects you will probably use direct quotes more frequently, and will need to discuss the quotes at length, and so you should ensure these are in quotation marks and clearly referenced.

It is important you don't just list papers you have found one after another, as this is not an annotated bibliography; instead you need to synthesise the information, pulling similar papers together where relevant. It is far better to group multiple authors and paraphrase a summary of their findings e.g.:

'There are many authors who support this approach (Chen et al., 2024; Fratelli & Green, 2022; Pinkerton, 2023), however...'

Students often ask how many references they need for their literature review, but unfortunately there is no simple answer to this question. In the sciences a typical 8,000 word dissertation may contain around 30–40 references, but this can vary depending on the subject and topic of the dissertation, and other subject areas could ask you to focus on, say, 10 significant pieces of work. Some dissertations may be in subject areas where there are vast quantities of published papers, and you cannot read everything; where this is the case you will need to refine your search terms to be more focused. For example, perhaps you could only look at research that uses the same methodologies as you, or studies on people of a particular age range, or only papers published in the last five years; such a focus should reduce the amount of papers you need to review. To begin with only skim read the papers to find out if they are relevant, then if they are suitable you can read them in more detail later.

Alternatively where there are few papers on your dissertation topic, particularly if you have found a gap in the literature, then you may need to look more widely and consider parallel studies. Perhaps you could look at similar studies that have employed different methodologies. Sometimes looking in cross-disciplinary subject areas can help. For example, if your study was on inflammation following injury in athletes, there may not be many papers in the sport science literature, however there will be lots of papers on inflammation in the biomedical and immunology journals. As mentioned previously, if you have found one really good paper, then have a look at the references the authors' cited. However, try not to over rely on a single source, as if this paper contained anything controversial or presented information not replicated elsewhere, it could skew your literature review; far better to present a variety of references to ensure you have represented the literature fairly and are presenting the full picture. If you are still having trouble identifying suitable references, then do speak to your dissertation supervisor as they may be able to point you to some suitable sources.

Do ensure that the references you use are good-quality sources. You are probably going to mostly rely on journal papers and books, although some textbooks may not be up to date enough for the research you are conducting. There may be key reports or data you need to refer to but avoid low-quality websites and information that is not evidence based.

Don't worry too much about the total number of references; as always quality is going to be more important that quantity. Your supervisor will be more focused on ensuring that what you write is evidence based and referenced appropriately, rather than counting how many references you have used.

At the end of the chapter

At the end of your literature review, you may want to provide a summary of the chapter, highlighting any controversies, including agreements and disagreements, and any gaps in the literature. You can also summarise any conclusions that can be drawn at this point. You may then want to clarify how your dissertation aims to fill any existing gaps in knowledge or extend what is known about your field of research.

Top tip from a student 17.1

Make sure you do your references as you go along when writing your literature review, or at least keep a note of the papers that you use; this will make it easier if you need to double check anything later and will make doing the reference list much easier. Kesha

---

Chapter summary

Your literature review chapter should summarise all the research previously conducted on your dissertation topic, and identify where there are controversies or gaps in the literature. It is important you provide an in-depth critique of the studies you are reporting and present a strong academic argument. Search the literature with focus, expanding your search only if you are struggling to find papers on your topic. Group similar papers and findings together and use these groupings to help plan the thematic structure of your literature review chapter; although depending on the subject you may also want to consider organising your literature review chronologically. You should find out if you are expected to present a theoretical framework as part of your literature review, as not all subject areas will require this. Reference high-quality sources as you go, and try not to over rely on single texts. At the end of the chapter summarise the findings so far and clearly articulate how your research aims to extend the work in this area.

Check list

- Your review of the literature may start broad, but then it will narrow and get more specific as you provide depth and detail about your area of study
- Make notes on the papers you read and try to group together papers that are similar
- Plan the structure of your literature review

- Remember, don't just report or describe each paper, but critique them
- Highlight any existing gaps in the literature
- Keep track of all the references that you use

Further reading

Bingham, A.J., Mitchell, R. and Carter, D.S. (2024) *A Practical Guide to Theoretical Frameworks for Social Science Research*. Philadelphia: Routledge.
Hart, C. (2018) *Doing a Literature Review*. London: Sage.

18

Writing the Methodology

Introduction

The methodology chapter is an important chapter as it describes how you collected and analysed your data, so that anyone could follow and replicate your methods if they so wished. For this reason methodologies need to be clear and concise, but they also need to be precise, and include every little detail about what you did and the order in which you did it. As well as describing your data collection methods, this chapter should also address how you analysed your data and, most importantly, how you ensured your study was ethical and safe.

The words 'methods' and 'methodology' are often used interchangeably but they do differ slightly in their meaning. Methodology generally refers to the theoretical reasoning and analysis of the methods that are used, whereas methods are more about how the data was collected. Therefore in a research paper or a practical report, where the authors are describing what they did, the term 'methods' is probably correct. However, in a dissertation where you are considering the overall approach and rationale for your study, 'methodology' is probably most appropriate.

The methodology chapter comes right after the literature review and therefore continues to justify the methodology you have chosen, but will add much more detail on the exact procedures. Although the methodology follows the literature review, it is important to keep your methods contained to the methodology chapter alone; don't let them creep out into other sections such as the introduction or the results (Hotaling, 2020).

Writing methodologies

Methodologies should always be written in the past tense, as you are describing the work that has been completed, for example:

- A total of 15 restaurants **were** surveyed
- The resulting solution **was** decanted into a test tube
- The interview **was** recorded using a voice recorder app and transcribed
- The results **were** collated on Excel
- All statistical comparisons **were** run in R version 4.3

You might have heard that methods should be written like recipes, however this is not strictly true. Whilst both methodologies and recipes may provide detailed descriptions, recipes are written in the active tense, telling you what to do, for example 'put the eggs into a bowl', whereas methodologies are written in the past tense, describing what happened, e.g. 'the eggs were put into a bowl'. Where possible also try to use the passive voice, so rather than writing 'I put the eggs into a bowl' you would write 'the eggs were put into a bowl'.

You want your methodology chapter to be concise, but you also want to ensure it contains adequate detail so the procedures you followed are clear.

It is also perfectly fine to cite references in your methodology chapter, particularly where you are following particular protocols, or to add support for the methods you chose to use to collect your research data.

Structure of a methodology chapter

A good way to start the methodology chapter is to restate your research question; this helps put into context the methods that you will be using. Then most methodologies will include the following information:

- The setting
- Date and duration of the study
- Study design
- Materials and apparatus used
- Sample
- Participants
- Procedure
- Ethical approval including informed consent, and a health and safety risk assessment
- Data analysis

These are described in detail below.

The setting – was your study a laboratory experiment or did it take place in a museum, a clinic or a school, etc., and who provided permission? If you completed fieldwork for a biological, geological or geographical project you would be expected to give a bit more detail about the location, the environment, the weather, temperature, even resource availability.

Date and duration of the study – you can simply state when the data was collected, or the start date and how long the study lasted, e.g. 'data collection commenced on 2 April 2024 and was completed over a period of three weeks'.

Study design – the study design is the overarching approach or framework that you have taken for your study in order to collect your data, i.e. what sort of research study did you do? This could be whether your study is empirical, quantitative or qualitative, or mixed methods, but more specifically the study type e.g. experimental, a randomised controlled trial, an observational study, a cross-sectional study, narrative research, case study, etc. If there is a rationale for your choice of study design then you should state that here too. You can read more about study design and the hierarchy of research design and evidence later in this chapter.

You can also define your key variables in the study design section of your methodology; notably the dependent, independent and controlled variables. The dependent variables are those that are being measured and that may be dependent on other variables, whereas the independent variables are those than can be manipulated (changed) for your experiment. Controlled variables are those that you keep constant.

Materials and apparatus used – you should give details of any equipment that was used, you can also list any reagents used, or if you were doing a survey you could list the questionnaires that you distributed or the audio recorder equipment that was used. If this is quite extensive you can always provide a full list in the appendix of your dissertation. When giving details about the equipment that were used, you should present the full name and also the name of the company that manufactured it and where they are located, e.g. 'Participants wore heart rate monitors (Polar Electro Ltd., Kempele, Finland).'

Sample – clarify what your samples were and how they were obtained and stored. 'n' is often used to represent the sample size e.g. 'The goats ($n = 4$) were observed whilst feeding.'

If your sample involved human participants, see below.

Participants – remember that the word 'participants' should always be used in preference to 'subjects', because rather than subjecting people to our research we ask them to participate, so for ethical reasons it is appropriate to refer to those that help our research as participants (Boynton, 1998). When it comes to participants, you should say who they were, and report how they were recruited and how many were recruited e.g. 'Twelve people (female $n = 7$; male $n = 5$) living with type 2 diabetes were recruited from a community clinic in a rural area of South Devon.'

It can be difficult to know how many participants you need to recruit. For an undergraduate level dissertation this may be opportunistic, or perhaps you have looked at previous studies to see how many people they have recruited and have used that as a guide. But the best way to determine how many participants you need for your study is to do a power calculation. A power calculation uses previously published data to estimate how many participants are needed to detect an effect, and there are now lots of computer packages that can do the calculations for you (Rudestam & Norton, 2014). For more on this see Jones et al. (2003) in the Further Reading section at the end of this chapter.

Procedure – describe the chronological order of events that took place, and how precisely the data were collected, e.g. 'participants were given information sheets, then were invited to provide informed consent, before completing the Dutch Eating Behaviour questionnaire.'

Alternatively, here is an example of a laboratory-based study procedure: 'blood samples were labelled and then centrifuged to separate the serum and plasma before they were pipetted into 5 ml vials and put into the ultralow freezer.'

If you are following a protocol that has been previously published you should make sure that you reference this, noting any changes that you made to the established protocol and why.

Ethical approval including informed consent, and health and safety risk assessment – these forms have all been described extensively in Chapter 15, as they need to be put in place before you can even start your dissertation. Essentially, any study that includes animals, humans or any sort of personal data or products from animals or humans, requires ethical approval. In your methods section, you should state who provided the ethical approval, the date it was approved and a reference number if there is one e.g.: 'Ethical approval was granted from the University of Greater London Ethics Committee on 4 June 2024 (Reference: LHSC 54/ 149).' You may also want to include the ethics form in the appendix of your dissertation.

If your study included human participants, you should ensure all participants agreed and provided informed consent, and then you can state 'that all participants signed informed consent forms, and a copy of a blank consent form can be found in the appendix'. Do make sure the consent form in the appendix is a blank one; all signed consent forms need to be stored securely to protect the anonymity of the participants. Likewise, if you completed a health and safety risk assessment you can state this '…was completed and a copy can be found in the appendix.'

It is also common to state if your study conforms to any national or international ethical standards such as the Declaration of Helsinki (World Medical Association, 2022).

Data analysis – this section is usually the last section of the methodology chapter, and should explain how you collated the data you collected, and how it was organised and analysed.

If your study was qualitative you will need to describe how you organised any information you collected including how you recorded and transcribed your data, if you coded it and if there were any forms of analysis such as thematic analysis or narrative analysis.

If you were doing a quantitative study, you should ensure you give the details of any statistical tests performed on the data and the software packages that were used e.g. 'Data were collated and analysed using SPSS version 30 (IBM Corp., Armonk, NY). The data were compared using an independent t test, a significance level of $p < 0.05$ was adopted.'

When writing your methodology chapter it can be really helpful to use these headings, as outlined above, to help you organise your material into the right paragraphs. You can also remove the paragraph headings later if you or your supervisor prefers.

More on study design

When writing about what method you used, you need to show how the methods you chose have answered your particular research questions.

Firstly, you will want to explain if your dissertation was empirical. An empirical study is one where you observed or measured something, whereas a non-empirical study does not include collecting any data, but instead focuses on summaries of the literature, methodologies or theories.

You should also clarify if your dissertation was qualitative or quantitative or mixed methods. Qualitative research collects data that is not numeric, but instead it is the rich information that can be gathered through focus groups and or interviews that would be impossible to put a number on. Conversely, quantitative data is numeric data that essentially can be counted or measured. Mixed methods is where the research being conducted encompasses both quantitative and qualitative methods, utilising the strengths that both types of research can offer, in order to answer a particular research question in greater depth.

Although there are many types of qualitative study, five of the mostly commonly used according to Cresswell and Poth (2024) are:

Phenomenology – a type of study that focuses on the individual's lived experiences, and how they understand those experiences within the world (Neubauer et al., 2019).

Grounded theory – the development of theories based on analysis of data that have been collected to get a richer or deeper understanding of particular complex phenomena.

179

Case study – exploration of a particular phenomenon using a variety of data sources and considers different lenses to fully understand the different facets of the phenomenon (Baxter & Jack, 2008).

Ethnography – studies that consider how communities, organisations and groups work, behave and interact together (Reeves, 2008).

Narrative research – usually based on interviews or histories, narratives tell a story about individual people or small groups and their experiences.

Likewise there are many types of quantitative studies that include:

Case reports – similar to the qualitative case study, a case report is an in-depth study of a particular individual, but when done quantitatively it will include data collection and analysis.

Surveys – a study that involves collecting data from many participants often via a questionnaire, asking questions and analysing the data.

Case control studies – where a group of participants are selected based on the phenomenon of interest, for example people living with osteoporosis, they are known as the cases and are compared to the controls, participants without the phenomenon of interest (in this example people who do not have osteoporosis). Historical factors are then investigated to see if there are certain features that are more common in the case participants compared to the control participants.

Cohort studies – longitudinal studies that follow a group of participants; over time any changes in disease incidence or even mortality are recorded.

Cross-sectional studies – gather information from a defined population and provide a snapshot of information at a given point in time.

Ecological studies – measure exposure and or disease in a population or community and look for relationships or correlations between the environment and particular outcome measures.

Experimental studies and interventions – investigators in these sorts of study manipulate or intervene to affect the outcome e.g. growing crops in soils with different mineral contents, or giving one group of participants an exercise programme to follow. These experiments and interventions should always include a control group.

Randomised controlled trial (RCT) – this is where the samples or participants are randomly assigned to be in the experimental or control group, and the outcomes of both groups are compared.

Systematic reviews – although similar to a literature review, this type of study reviews existing published data and attempts to synthesize all the evidence on a particular topic in order to answer a pre-determined research question. In order to find appropriate material, the literature is searched systematically with pre-defined criteria to ensure all relevant studies are included and to avoid the risk of bias.

Meta-analyses –similar to systematic reviews, but in this case all the data from the relevant studies are re-analysed statistically, commonly using a forest plot, in order to pool the data, and reduce the potential for error from individual studies.

Clearly there are a lot of different study types to consider. But you may also want to take into account how strong the evidence is from the different types of research study. Figure 18.1 describes the hierarchy of study design and evidence, starting at the top with the strongest forms of evidence right down to the weakest.

Strength of evidence	Type of study
Strongest	Meta-analyses and systematic reviews
	Randomised controlled trial
	Cohort studies
	Case control studies
	Case reports
Weakest	Opinions and anecdotes

Figure 18.1 Hierarchy of study design and evidence

Although you may have used a method that is not one of the strongest types, your study can still be important and can even be a good starting point for stronger studies later. However, it is important that you are aware of the limitations of the methods you have chosen and you will want to explore that further in the discussion chapter of your dissertation.

Pilot and feasibility testing

It would probably be quite unusual to do a pilot test as part of an undergraduate dissertation, given the limited amount of time available, but if you did trial your research protocol on a smaller scale, or did some form of feasibility study before fully launching, you could classify that as a pilot study. In fact trialling your study is probably a good idea, since you can check that you are happy with the protocols and confident with the techniques required. Pilot studies should be reported in the methods chapter, and kept separate from your main results. If your pilot study resulted in any changes to your protocol or the materials or questionnaires that you used in your main study, then you should report that here too.

Methodologies if your dissertation is literature-based

Even if you are doing a project that does not involve an experiment or an intervention, but is based on the literature, such as a narrative review, you can still write a methodology section, although it may be quite brief. Here you should describe the search terms that you used to find relevant literature, or if your search involved any inclusion or exclusion criteria, for example: 'only including quantitative studies on adults with work related stress, but excluding any qualitative studies, or studies on adults with other forms of stress.' You can also give the time frame, for example, 'papers published between 1 January 1994 and 1 October 2024.' The search engines that you used to find papers should be listed too, for example 'Google Scholar and Scopus.' You can list any other method you used to find information for your dissertation.

You can also outline any philosophical approach you took, and if you used a particular theoretical or conceptual framework to structure your dissertation then you may also want to refer back to that too. You should also explain how your methods linked to your research question, how you dealt with the information you found, how it was recorded, and if any data analysis or organisation was completed.

It is also worth noting that in some subject areas, notably English language and literature, the dissertation does not include a methodology chapter at all; instead there is an extended literature review. If you are in any way unsure what is expected in your subject area, do talk to your dissertation supervisor for confirmation.

Top tip from a student 18.1

Because I had already done a really detailed ethics form, writing the methodology chapter was actually quite easy, I just had to remember to put it all in the past tense. Ron

---

Chapter summary

There is a lot of information you need to include in the methodology section, but by following the recommended structure you can ensure you don't miss out any crucial details. It is really important you provide details on the setting of your study, the date and duration of the study, your chosen study design and what equipment you used to collect your data. Samples and participant groups all need to be described, including how you recruited participants and how informed consent was confirmed. You should already have your ethics forms and health and safety forms completed but it is important to refer to them in your methods too. Lastly, you should clearly describe how you analysed your data in detail. Even if your study was literature-based you may still be expected to describe how and when you collected your information.

Check list

- Check the expectations for a methodology chapter in your subject area
- If you are required to write a methodology chapter, follow the typical structure for a methodology chapter to ensure you don't leave out any important sections
- Double check you have information on the setting, the date, the study design, any materials used, that you have described your sample and/or participants, the ethics, and how you analysed your data
- Have you put the relevant forms and questionnaires in the appendix of your dissertation?
- Have you provided enough detail so that another researcher could replicate your study?

Further reading

Anderson, E.E. and Corneli, A.L. (2018) *100 Questions (and Answers) about Research Ethics*. London: Sage.

Jones, S.R., Carley, S. and Harrison, M. (2003) An introduction to power and sample size estimation. *Emergency Medicine Journal*, 20: 453–458.

19

Planning the Results Chapter

Introduction

The results chapter is probably one of the most important chapters in your dissertation, since it is where you present the findings of your research and see the results of all the hard work you put into collecting and analysing your data. Results chapters need to present your data in the best possible format, and that includes a clear explanation of any statistical tests that were performed, alongside well-presented tables and graphs. If you did a qualitative study you will want to ensure that the key themes and quotes are presented neatly and are anchored and explained in detail. It is also worth noting that not all subject areas expect a chapter of results as part of the dissertation, so do take the time to check what is expected in your subject area.

When writing your results chapter, you will want to be as clear as possible, but also write in a concise style and objective manner. At this point in your dissertation you are simply presenting your findings and not discussing them. You will want to present your results in a logical manner so that the chapter flows. You can do this in the same order that you described the procedure in your methodology, or you can organise your findings chronologically. If you used mixed methods you might want to divide the results into the different methods used, or you can organise your results in response to your initial research questions or hypotheses (Joyner et al., 2018).

Tables and graphs should all be titled and numbered, but when we title and number a graph we usually refer to it as a figure. Figures include not only graphs, but charts, maps, photos and images too. You should also make sure you refer to any tables and figures in the text, and describe what they show.

You should write your results chapter in the past tense, but there may be times when you need to refer to a table or a graph, in which case it is fine to use the present tense, for example 'Figure 1 shows...'

Quantitative data

It is usual to only present processed or aggregated data in the results chapter. Any individual results or raw data should be put in the appendix (unless your dissertation is an individual case study). Usually we present data in the form of averages, in particular the mean or the median; results presented as raw data are shown in Table 19.1, however a table like this should really go in the appendix, and instead you should present your data after it has been processed as shown in Table 19.2.

Table 19.1 Example of raw data

Sample	Soil type	Plant height (cm)
1	Clay	5.6
2	Clay	5.2
3	Clay	4.9
4	Clay	5.5
5	Chalk	3.2
6	Chalk	3.4
7	Chalk	4.0
8	Chalk	3.0

It would be usual to take your raw data and calculate the mean and standard deviation (SD) for all samples in each group, and then the data could be presented in the processed form, as shown in Table 19.2.

Table 19.2 The processed data

Soil type	n	Plant height (cm) mean ± SD
Clay	4	5.3 ± 0.3
Chalk	4	3.4 ± 0.4

Where n = the sample size, SD = standard deviation

The mean is calculated by adding up all the numbers in a data set and then dividing the number of data points that you have. Anywhere you present a mean value it is good practice to also present the standard deviation, as this gives an indication of how spread out the data in the group is from the average figure.

If your data is not normally distributed, then it would be more appropriate to present the median value, i.e. the middle value in a set of data. Instead of a standard deviation, the median is usually presented in conjunction with the interquartile range, which gives an indication of the spread of the middle half of the distribution of your data.

Mean, standard deviation, median and interquartile range can all be described as descriptive statistics and can be easily calculated using Excel or any statistical software package such as SPSS, R, Stata, SAS, MATLAB, etc.

Statistical tests are going to be key to analysing any quantitative data, and some commonly used tests are described in Table 19.3. The actual performing of statistical tests is beyond the scope of this book on writing skills, but there are suggestions for appropriate books in the Further Reading section at the end of this chapter.

Table 19.3 Types of common statistical tests

Tests to see if your data is normally distributed (or parametric)	
Kolmogorov–Smirnov test	Test for normality for large numbers of samples
Shapiro–Wilk test	Test for normality for small numbers of samples
Tests that look for differences	
T-test	Compares two sets of data (parametric)
Paired t-test	Compares data from the same group in two different conditions (parametric)
Analysis of variance (ANOVA)	Compares more than two groups (parametric)
Mann-Whitney U-test	Compares two independent groups (non-parametric)
Kruskal–Wallis test	Compares two or more groups (non-parametric)
Tests for relationships	
Pearson's correlation	Looks for correlations between two sets of data (parametric)
Spearman's correlation	Looks for correlations between two sets of data (non-parametric)

Your raw statistics files can go in the appendix, but there is some data you will want to include in the results tables. It is usual to present the test statistic, for example if you are doing a t-test, this is the figure known as t, or the F if you are doing an ANOVA, or if you are doing a correlation, it is the correlation coefficient r. But it is also usual to present the p value. There are lots of debates about p values, but generally p represents probability and is often used to indicate statistical significance. You might have seen $p < 0.05$ on research papers you have read, and typically if p is less than 0.05 then usually this means that there is a significant difference or that the relationship is significant. However, there are lots of debates on how to interpret statistical significance and some authors recommend presenting confidence intervals as well; for further reading see Greenland et al. (2016).

Tables

A table is often the clearest way to present data, particularly if you have a lot of detailed data that could be difficult to follow when written in the text, or read precisely from a graph. Data should be in summarised form, and both the columns and the rows should have clear headings, so it is easy to understand the data being presented at a glance. Tables should have a number and a title, and this should be above the tables.

There are options for the horizontal and vertical lines and shading in your table, but don't overdo them; in fact many journals recommend that tables of data should only include horizontal lines, and no shading, so you might want to replicate that style in your dissertation; see the examples in Tables 19.4 and 19.5 that describe the characteristics of participants in a fictional study investigating cholesterol levels. Which table do you think is clearer and more professional looking?

Table 19.4 Example of data in a heavily formatted table, with contrast row shading and bold column and row heading text

Characteristics	Mean	Standard deviation
Age (years)	51	3.7
Height (m)	1.68	0.07
Weight (kg)	68	9.5
Cholesterol (mg/dL)	215	32
HDL cholesterol (mg/dL)	110	25
LDL cholesterol (mg/dL)	50	12

Table 19.5 Example of data in a minimally formatted table, with horizontal lines for only the header row and no shading

Characteristics	Mean	Standard deviation
Age (years)	51	3.7
Height (m)	1.68	0.07
Weight (kg)	68	9.5
Cholesterol (mg/dL)	215	32
HDL cholesterol, (mg/dL)	110	25
LDL cholesterol, (mg/dL)	50	12

Graphs

Try to avoid replicating data, so if you have presented your results in a table, there is no need to present the same data in the form of a graph; just ensure you choose the best format for presenting the data clearly.

Microsoft Excel is commonly used to create graphs, and this is on most computers; it is easy to use, and to change the colours and label your graphs. But you can use other packages such as Canva, Adobe Illustrator, GraphPad, Prism, etc. or even some statistical packages if you prefer. Find out what packages your university has access to, and which ones produce the best graphs for your needs.

Choosing the most appropriate graph is essential, since not all graphs suit all sorts of data. Figure 19.1 provides a reminder of the four main types of graph and what they are best used to display.

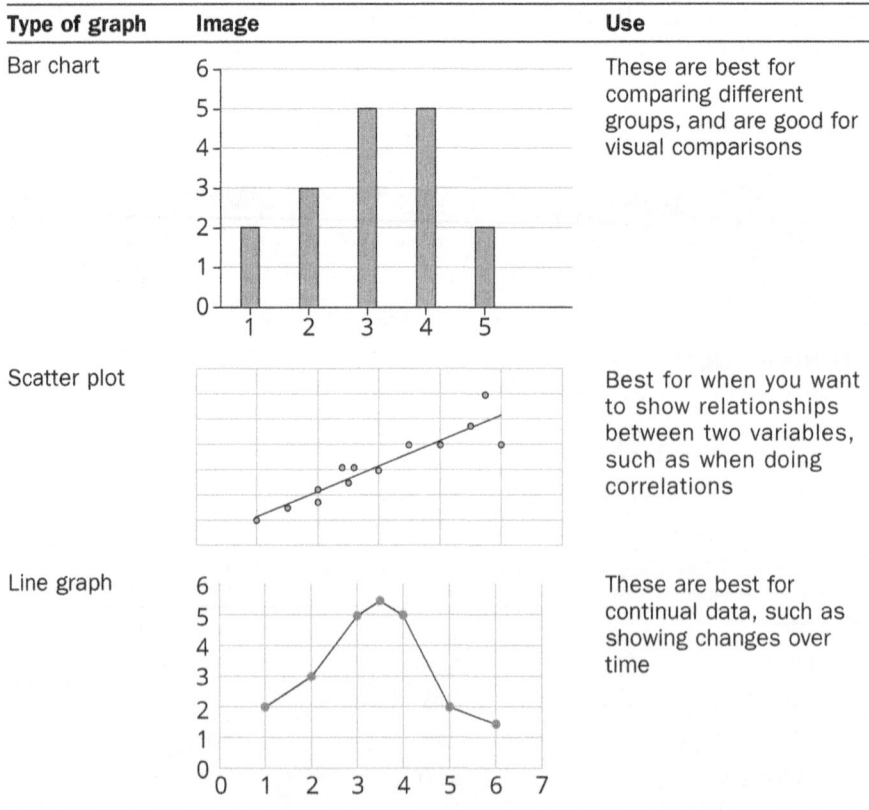

Type of graph	Image	Use
Bar chart		These are best for comparing different groups, and are good for visual comparisons
Scatter plot		Best for when you want to show relationships between two variables, such as when doing correlations
Line graph		These are best for continual data, such as showing changes over time

Type of graph	Image	Use
Pie chart		Pie charts can be used when all the parts add up to a whole; they are often used to show percentages

Figure 19.1 Graph type and use

When you have decided on which type of graph to display your data, you also need to consider how best to display the data within the graph. Figure 19.2 shows the same data but depicted on graphs with different axes. On graph a) the x axis is expanded, whereas on graph b) the x axis fits the data better and as a result you can see the relationship between temperature and growth rate clearer. Changing the axes of your graphs and setting different minimum and maximums can make the presentation look very different, so change the axes as necessary in order to show the data to its best advantage.

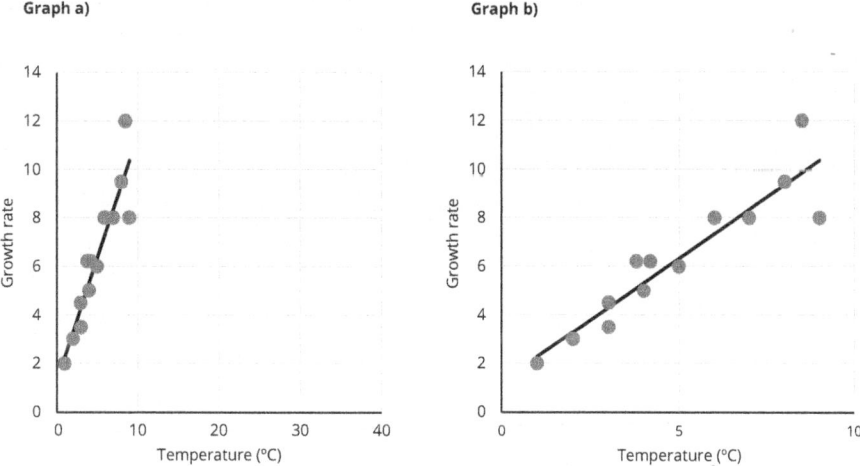

Figure 19.2 Graphs with data presented on different axes (adapted from Jeanes, 2022)

The axis should be labelled and the units of measurement included, and the graph should have a number and title. The figure numbers and titles are usually put beneath the figure, unlike tables where the title is usually at the top.

If you are including a graph such as a pie chart, you might want to colour code it, and therefore you will need to have a key, so it is clear which colour represents which group. When creating graphs it is easy to change the colours and make them bright and interesting, but don't get too carried away with clashing colours or colours that are hard to distinguish between, as your graph could end up looking gaudy or unclear. Instead go for complementary colours or even stick to black, white and grey-scale.

Presenting qualitative data

Qualitative research provides data that cannot be represented numerically and therefore often includes the presentation of analysis-generated themes, and quotations that illustrate those themes; these are outlined below.

Thematic analysis is a popular research methodology for qualitative research, and if this is a technique you have used, you will need to be able to present the themes you have identified. You could use your key themes as paragraph headings to help organise your results chapter. Alternatively, if they are just one part of the chapter then you could just list them in the text, or you can tabulate them to make them stand out. A table is also a really good way of summarising your findings.

An example of a table showing key themes and quotes from a fictional qualitative study investigating why people go for walks in a community park is shown in Table 19.6.

Table 19.6 An example of a table showing themes and key quotes

Pre-determined areas of investigation	Themes	Key quotes
Reasons to walk	Exercise	'I feel better when I do exercise'
	Stress relief	'After work I enjoy the walk home to clear my head'
	Pets	'Well if you have a dog you have to walk it don't you'
Etc.		

If you wanted to expand Table 19.6 further, you could have an additional column, for 'Explanation' or 'Meaning' where you could briefly explain or put the quotes into context. If using tables do make sure to use the exact same headings that you use in the narrative part of your results so as not to confuse the reader (Cooper, 2018).

Alternatively you can present the themes as an image. SmartArt on Microsoft Word is an easy way to insert and present visual images. Figure 19.3 uses SmartArt to present the key themes that came out of a fictional study of a focus group discussing barriers to a healthy diet.

Don't spend too long creating images and playing with the SmartArt feature, after all it is the content and your findings that are the most important things. Neither tables nor images should be in isolation, they are just there to provide an overview; in addition you must ensure you fully describe the findings presented and provide more detail and context.

As mentioned, qualitative data often includes the presentation of quotes, and the quotes are your raw data, which you can use to illustrate your points or the themes you have identified to provide deeper understanding. It is important you don't just list your quotes, instead you need to compile, analyse and explain them (Anderson, 2010). It is important to anchor your quotes and to explain what you think the quotes are illustrating. For example, if you were conducting a qualitative study on social media use by university students, you might put all quotes that mention fake news together and introduce the quote as follows:

Participants showed awareness of the propensity for fake news on social media:

'I don't believe everything I read, even the photos are edited, I try to take it all with a pinch of salt.' (22 years old)

You could then add more quotes, or move on to the next theme.

Pick the quotes that reflect the patterns and themes that you see in your data. Make sure your quotes are not too long, you don't want to

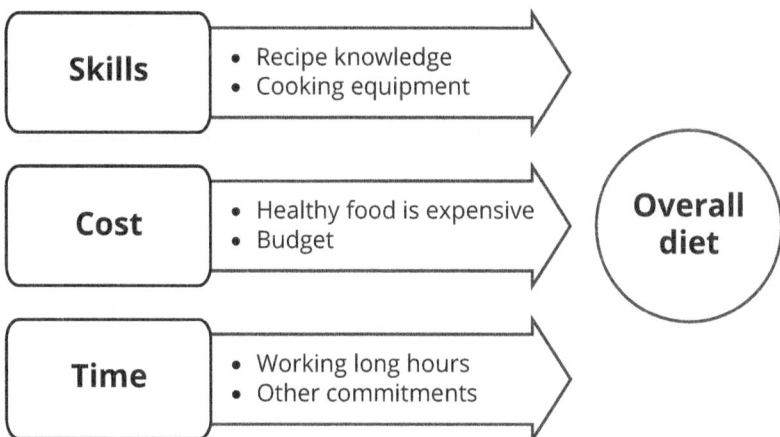

Figure 19.3 An example of using SmartArt to present key themes

write out the entire transcript, but perhaps if you do have a long quote that is really important you could break it up into different parts that you can explain separately. Always ensure your quotes are presented accurately and objectively. Although you are contextualising and organising them, you should never make any judgements, and you should save any discussion of the quotes for the discussion chapter. However, you do need to ensure that you provide enough information about the quotes that you use, so the findings can be put into context.

There is no set number of quotes that you should include. Try to find some key quotes for each theme and add any you think contain key details you need to explore. You can also summarise your findings where possible, for example: '6 out of the 8 participants mentioned…'

Remember, like any data you present in your dissertation, your findings should be anonymous and so your quotes should be too, so either use a code name or some form of pseudonym, for example:. 'female participant 1.'

Findings

In some subject areas, such as law, rather than having a results chapter, there is a chapter on findings. The findings chapter is essentially the same as a results chapter but often for non-empirical dissertations that are based on published reports and literature. Like in the results chapter, here you should provide an overview of your main findings. You can use graphs and tables as appropriate to pool and summarise your findings.

You may also want to organise the chapter into the key themes that you have identified; this can be according to any framework you have proposed earlier in the thesis, or even chronologically, but you want the chapter to have a coherent structure and flow from one theme to another. Using paragraph headings can be a useful way of structuring and organising your information.

At the end of your results or findings chapter, it is useful to summarise what you have found and presented.

Dissertations in arts-based subjects

In some subject areas, such as English language and literature, the dissertation does not include a results chapter at all, instead the literature review is expansive and includes all the major findings and critical analysis directly from the literature. You will still need to source evidence and present different academic arguments, as with all critical writing, and you should also try to organise your information into sections with a logical structure, but there will be no data as such. If you are in anyway unsure what is expected in your subject area, as always do talk to your dissertation supervisor for confirmation.

> ## Top tip from a student 19.1
>
> *Don't put off doing your statistics to the end, you have to do them at some point, and if you get them done it will make writing the other chapters easier.* Amos

Chapter summary

Results chapters need be clear and detailed to ensure you present enough data to answer your research questions. The data should be processed, with raw data being put into the appendix. Think carefully how to present your data to the best advantage, whether that is in a table, a graph or even using SmartArt, to ensure it is clear but not so elaborate that it detracts from the content. Introduce any themes and anchor the quotations, don't just cut and paste them into the chapter, as they need to be analysed and explained. Remember in the results chapter you are just presenting your data, not discussing it; save that for the next chapter, the discussion. At the end of the chapter summarise your key findings.

Finally, please be aware that not all subject areas include a results chapter as part of the dissertation; it may be called a 'findings' chapter, or there may not be one if the dissertation is entirely literature based. Do speak to your dissertation supervisor about what is expected in your subject area.

Check list

- Have you chosen the best way to present your data and is it clear and easy to read?
- Have you analysed your data appropriately?
- If you had quantitative data did you choose the correct statistical test?
- If you had qualitative data have you transcribed and analysed your data with the appropriate technique?

- Do the tables and figures have titles and labels?
- Are the tables and figures described and explained in the text?
- Check you have presented enough data to answer your research question
- Have you summarised your key findings?

Further reading

Greenland, S., Senn, S.J., Rothman, K.J., Carlin, J.B., Poole, C., Goodman, S.N. and Altman, D.G. (2016) Statistical tests, P values, confidence intervals, and power: A guide to misinterpretations. *European Journal of Epidemiology*, 31: 337–350.

Pallant, J. (2020) *SPSS Survival Manual: A Step By Step Guide to Data Analysis Using IBM SPSS*. 7th edition. London: McGraw-Hill Education; Open University Press.

Schmuller, J. (2017) *Statistical Analysis with R for Dummies*. Wiley: New Jersey.

20

Discussions and Conclusions

Introduction

The discussion chapter is where you delve into your results, explore their meanings and put them into context. You will be selecting key results to discuss, critiquing your own findings and comparing your results to the literature, as you develop and strengthen your academic arguments and present the evidence for your original hypotheses, putting all your critical analysis skills to good use. This is also where you can reflect on your results, highlight the strengths and limitations of your study and consider what further research is needed.

The final conclusion to your dissertation can be part of the discussion chapter, or a chapter in its own right, and both options will be discussed here.

The discussion

The discussion is an opportunity for you to provide an in-depth analysis of your findings, critique your own study, and essentially bring together all the previous chapters, since you will be revisiting your research questions, the literature you critiqued, the methodologies you used, and the results you presented.

Although you will be returning to the literature you presented earlier, it's important that your discussions do not become a repeat of your introduction or literature review, as this time you will need to explain the relevance of your results and show how your research has furthered the field of study. What new insights has your data brought, has it verified other research, or filled any of the knowledge gaps, perhaps your data has even revealed new gaps?

You will be critiquing the methodology that you used, but you won't be explaining how the methods were performed.

Similarly, the discussion should not simply be a repeat of the results chapter, nor should you bring in new findings here. Instead, it is your opportunity to reflect on your findings in depth, compare them to existing research, understand their strengths and limitations, and consider the context of your results and how your work can be applied.

Knowing the tense in which to write the discussion can be slightly challenging, since you are likely to use a mixture of tenses. When you discuss your methods or your results you should use the past tense, however when you are putting your findings into context and making current comparisons you should use the present tense. Then when you make recommendations for further research you can use the future tense. For example:

'The results of the survey found that there was a reduction in...' (past)

'This finding concurs with Smith (2024) and appears to suggest...' (present)

'It is recommended that further research should investigate...' (future)

Take care with the language you use in the discussion and try to be circumspect rather than overly bold with your findings. It is rarely possible to prove something 100%, so for that reason you might want to present your arguments more cautiously, for example, using phrases such 'it is possible that...' or 'the reasons for this could be...' rather than making statements of absolute certainty or over generalising.

When it comes to the structure of the discussion chapter it is usually a good idea to try to use the same structure and follow the same order that you used in the results chapter; this will be the most logical and help the flow of information through your dissertation.

A typical structure for a dissertation would be as follows:

- A summary of your key findings
  - o Including an explanation of what the results mean
- Comparisons with similar studies
  - o Add any theories or explanations as to why these studies may be different from yours
- Strengths and limitations of your study

- Recommendations
- Suggestions for further research
- Conclusion

More detail about the each of these sections is given below.

A summary of your key findings

Start with the more general findings before moving onto the more specific, following the same order as the results chapter. Don't bring in any new data here, all the data and findings should be in the results chapter, ready to be interpreted here. If your study identified themes in the results, you can discuss each one here in the same order that they were presented in the results chapter. Now is the time to explain what your results mean, and any explanations you have for why the results are what they are. It is also important that you explain any unexpected results, or null results (i.e. non-significant results). Although you will need to explain your results including the unexpected ones, this does not mean you need to discuss every single result; you need to be selective, and choose the key results, so as not to dilute your findings (Buczkowski, 2023b). For example, you may have done a survey that included eight questions, but perhaps not every question was critical to your overall research objectives; if this is the case then there is no need to discuss those questions that do not fulfil your objectives, however you will need to use all your analytical skills to ensure you do not miss discussing key results.

You should also return to your original research questions and hypotheses, reiterate these, and state how your findings have answered your research questions and if they support your hypotheses.

Comparisons with similar studies

You should look at similar studies in the literature, and you can return to some of the research you wrote about in your literature review here, and compare and contrast the findings from those papers to that of your study (University of York, 2024). You can also refer to any theories from the literature. Are the findings and theories similar to yours, do they agree with and support your findings? If so you can use phrases such as the following:

'The findings of this study are in agreement with Jones and Chan (2024) in that…'

'The results are consistent with the theory that…'

'Comparisons with earlier studies show similarities…'

197

Or if your results are different, and you offer a counter argument to the claims, you can use phrases such as:

'The findings of this study contradict earlier research…'

'Research by Ahmed and Johns (2025) reported a difference between the samples, however this was not replicated in the results presented here…'

'The theories previously presented do not appear to apply to this study…'

If your findings are different to previously published work, then you need to consider if there are particular reasons for this, for example perhaps they had different samples, different equipment, different analyses, etc. You need to defend your findings and explain why your results and inter-pretations may be different from the work of others, and this is where you can put into practice what you learnt in Chapter 4 of this book about how to construct an academic argument and use evidence:

1. Make your point
2. Present the evidence
3. Offer the counter argument
4. Summarise and draw your conclusions

Depending on the organisation of your discussion chapter and the num-ber of results and themes you need to discuss, you may want to combine the summaries of your key findings with the comparisons of similar studies. As such you could:

- Present one key result or theme
- Compare to previous studies and theories
- Provide your overall analysis

You can then repeat this for each key finding or theme, starting a new paragraph for each one.

Strengths and limitations of your study

It is important to highlight what your study did well: perhaps you had a strong framework, showed statistical rigour, and recruited a representa-tive sample. These strengths can be introduced with the following phrase:

'The study had several strengths...'

No study is ever perfect so there will always be some limitations to discuss, and you can introduce these similarly:

'The study had several limitations...'

Be critical, but not apologetic. Yes, your study would have been better if you had recruited hundreds more participants, but this would not have been realistic in the time-frame. Likewise, you may not have had access to state of the art instruments, but perhaps you did a sound study that was well controlled with the equipment that was available to you, so take care that you don't completely undermine all your hard work.

Recommendations

It is not always possible to make recommendations on the basis of your research; this may depend on your subject area, the topic of your dissertation and your particular findings. But if your results have led to new information that has specific applications you may be able to make recommendations and they can be reported towards the end of your discussion, but also in the conclusion too. If you can make recommendations, you will need to be clear who they are aimed at, such as other researchers, practitioners or perhaps governments. But crucially they must be based on evidence and backed by your research. In fact, your recommendation could just be that more research is needed.

Suggestions for further research

How would you do things differently, but just as importantly, what research would you do next, what gaps have opened up that now require further research. Perhaps there are clear applications for your work, and if you think your findings will influence policy or will influence practice in any way you should make that clear too.

Complete your discussion chapter with a concise summary of your findings and their implications, and how they answer your original research question.

Conclusion

The conclusion comes at the very end of the dissertation, and it might be the final section of your discussion chapter, or a chapter in its own right – this will depend on your subject area and the preferences of your supervisor.

If your conclusion is at the end of the discussion, it may only be one or two paragraphs. If it is a standalone chapter then it will be longer, however this is probably the shortest chapter in your dissertation, and so it still may only be two or three pages long.

Shape of the conclusion chapter

Do you recall the inverted pyramid used to represent your introduction chapter? Similarly, you can imagine the conclusion as the reverse, i.e. it is a pyramid but this time it is the right way round. For a visual image of the structure of the whole dissertation see Figure 20.1.

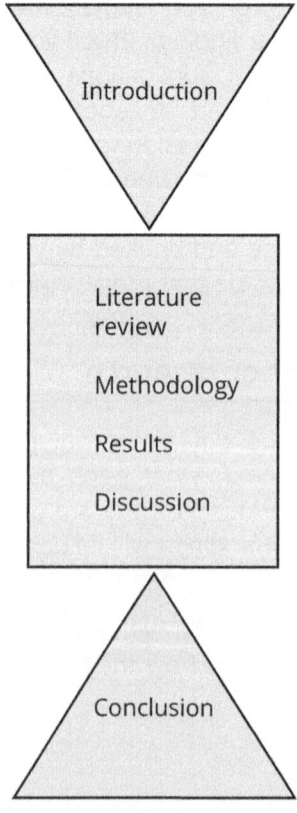

Figure 20.1 Visual image of the shape of a dissertation

The conclusion starts narrow, as you remind the reader of your specific research question (this is represented by the tip of the pyramid) where you summarise the results from your study. But then it will get broader as you put your findings into context and show their application in the widest sense, and demonstrate how they fit into the broader subject area. You can even return to the broader themes that you presented in your introduction in order to tie up all the loose ends and ensure there is cohesion throughout your dissertation. As such, the conclusion is not the place for new data or insights, since these should all have been presented in the preceding chapters. Instead, here you want to provide a logical conclusion to your dissertation that summarises and synthesises your overall findings, arguments, and recommendations, and puts them into context.

The conclusion should end with a concise but strong take home message. This could be the answer to your original research question, or a recap of the findings and implications, but essentially your take home message should be a clear and final statement about your research that you want to the reader to remember.

Top tip from a student 20.1

While writing the other chapters, particularly the results chapter, I would get ideas for what I wanted to explore in the discussion, and so I made a note of them. Then when I came to the discussion, I already had an outline of all the key points that I needed to discuss. Frida

---

Chapter summary

The discussion is all about explaining your results, comparing them with other studies and putting them into context, in light of your original research questions. You should highlight the strengths and limitations of your dissertation – no dissertation is perfect, and this can show that you understand the limits and the context of your research. If your research has implications for practice, or has made recommendations, or identified where further research is needed, you should highlight that too. Finally, a concise conclusion that synthesises and summarises your findings and presents a clear take home message will be the perfect end to your dissertation.

Check list

- Have you summarised your key results and explained what they mean?
- Have you compared your results with similar studies from the literature?
- Don't forget to report the strengths and limitations of your research
- Are there any recommendations, and have you suggested ideas for further research?
- Do you have a well-written conclusion that summarises your findings and puts your research into context?
- Make sure you have a clear take home message

Further reading

Reeves, S. and Buczkowski, B. (2023) *Mastering Your Dissertation*. Heidelberg: Springer.

21

Abstracts, Appendices, Editing and Proof Reading

Introduction

Once you have written all the chapters it might feel like all the hard work is out of the way, and this is true, but there are still a few final vital parts of the dissertation that you will need to complete. This chapter considers the front and end pieces of the dissertation including the title page, the abstract, the lists of contents and appendices, as well as the editing and proof reading required to ensure your dissertation is professional looking and ready for submission.

Even though you are almost at the end of the dissertation it is important to add the final elements and ensure the dissertation flows from the start to the end. The usual order for all the parts of a dissertation is given below:

- Title page
- Abstract
- Acknowledgements
- Contents
- List of tables and figures
- List of abbreviations
- Introduction
- Literature review
- Methodology
- Results/findings
- Discussion
- Conclusion
- References
- Bibliography (if required)
- Appendices

Title page

The first thing that will be seen is the title page, and so it needs to be presented well in order to make your dissertation look professional. Your university may provide a template or specific guidance as to what to include on your title page, but usually this will include:

- The title of your dissertation
- Your name (unless you have been asked to submit your work anonymously)
- Student ID number
- Your degree title
- The name of the department you are in
- Your university
- Date: month and year
- Your supervisor's name
- You may also be asked to add a statement such as: 'Dissertation submitted in partial fulfilment of the requirements for a bachelor's degree in [give your degree title here]'
- You may also be asked to add a statement declaring that the dissertation is all your own work e.g.: 'I declare that this dissertation is entirely my own work, except where referenced or acknowledged.'

However, this last statement is sometimes declared when you submit the work.

The text on the title page is usually centred, and the title is usually in a larger font than the rest of the information. An example of a template for a title page is shown in Box 21.1.

Box 21.1   A template for a dissertation title page

Dissertation title

By

[your name]

Student ID

Dissertation submitted in partial fulfilment of the requirements for a bachelor's degree in [give your degree title here]

Department name

University name

Month/year

Supervisor: name

The abstract

The abstract is last thing you write but will be the first thing that the reader reads (other than the title page), and therefore you want to ensure that it gives a strong but accurate account of the entire dissertation and sets the scene appropriately.

Abstracts can be structured or unstructured. A structured abstract is usually organised with the following paragraph headings:

Background

Objective

Method

Results

Conclusions

An unstructured abstract will contain the same information but without the formal paragraph headings.

Essentially the abstract needs to be written very concisely as you only have space to provide a few sentences summarising each chapter of your dissertation, with the exception of the discussion, which is not included here. You need to provide some background to the study from your introduction and literature review as a rationale for the research that was conducted, and present your aims and/or objectives. You should also add a brief summary of the main methods, stating the techniques you used. You only have space to include key results here and it is good to include some data if you can. There is no space for a discussion in the abstract, but you should include a conclusion to summarise your main findings.

The number of words for an abstract can vary between 150 and 500 words, but it should never be more than one page of A4.

Acknowledgements

Although optional and not marked, it is thoughtful to include some acknowledgements in your dissertation, and usually these are placed directly after the abstract and in front of the contents page. This is where you can express your thanks to the people that have helped with your dissertation and during your time at university. You should thank your supervisor for their input and support, perhaps your tutor, as well as any technicians, research assistants, statistics advisors, etc.

that helped you with your work. You may also want to thank your family and friends for their support, during the dissertation and your time at university. There may be lots of people you would like to thank but you should probably try and restrict this section to one, or a maximum of two, paragraphs.

Contents page

It is usual to have a contents page for a dissertation. However, some universities these days ask for work to be presented as a research paper rather than a thesis, and papers would rarely have a contents page.

Usually, you would state on which page you can find each chapter, and then also each section and or subheadings as follows:

Contents

Chapter..2

Heading 1...2

Subheading 2...3

If you are using Microsoft Word, it is possible to insert an automated contents page which will update automatically if the page numbers change. The built-in contents page can be found on the References tab on the toolbar, or search the help function for more details.

Although most dissertations have a contents page, they would rarely have an index page, so you won't need to worry about that.

In addition to a contents page, traditional dissertations also have a list of tables and a list of figures, or a combined list of tables and figures, that are set up similarly to the contents page and list every table and figure presented throughout the whole dissertation.

If you are working in a field where there are lots of abbreviations with the potential to cause confusion, you can also add an alphabetical list of abbreviations.

References lists and bibliographies

Hopefully you have been compiling your list of references as you went along, so now you just need to make sure they are presented neatly, are in the right order, and contain all the required details for whichever referencing system you have been asked to follow (see Chapter 5 if you need a reminder).

Some subject areas also ask for a bibliography, and this should be listed separately from the reference list. This is where you list any background or further reading you did, and name any resources that you used, that you didn't cite directly. It is usual to put any bibliographic sources in alphabetical order.

Appendices

This is the last section of the dissertation and is usually found after the references. Any additional or supplementary information that you need to support your dissertation can be put here. The sorts of documents you may want to put in the appendices include:

- Your raw data including any interview transcripts
- The statistical analysis, or any equations used
- Ethics form
- Health and safety risk assessment form
- Blank copy of the informed participant consent form
- Examples of any questionnaires that were used
- Letters of agreement
- Any additional information, such as handouts, recipes, full protocols or lists of reagents, etc.

Do make sure all your appendices are labelled, and usually with a letter, e.g.:

Appendix A: Participant consent form

Word counts

Word counts for dissertations can vary hugely between programmes and universities. Some courses may request the dissertation is written up like a journal paper, so it will have a word count of maybe 4,000 words, whereas another institution could ask for 10,000 or 15,000 words for a Master's thesis.

It is difficult to say how many words are required for each chapter, as again this may vary, but two examples are given in Table 21.1. Please note this is only a guide: it is the total word count that is the most important, not the word count for the individual chapters.

Table 21.1 Word count for each chapter in dissertations of different lengths

4,000 word dissertation	10,000 word dissertation
• Introduction and literature review – 1,000 words	• Introduction – 1,000 words
	• Literature review – 2,500 words
• Methods – 800 words	• Methodology – 1,500 words
• Results – 1,000 words	• Results – 2,000 words
• Discussion and conclusion – 1,200 words	• Discussion – 2,000 words
	• Conclusion – 1,000 words

Editing and proof reading

Make sure you leave plenty of time at the end for proof reading your dissertation and doing all the final checks.

You should ensure your dissertation is neatly presented and that you have used a clear and legible font such as Times New Roman, Arial or Calibri, and usually size 11 or 12. Double line spacing can also make your work look well-presented and is easier for the reader.

Spelling and grammar can be checked using the review functions on your computer, but this is no substitute for reading through the work yourself. As well as looking at spelling and punctuation, check for formatting, titles and labels, but also check for consistency and ensure you use the same terminology throughout. Look for repetition and remove any unnecessary words that can affect the conciseness of what you have written. For example, rather than saying 'data was collected on a weekly basis' (7 words), you could just state 'data was collected weekly' (4 words). However, don't skip over essential points, and ensure you do provide enough detail.

Try reading your work out loud or get your computer to read it out loud to you. This can help ensure that every sentence is structured correctly and that your writing flows well. Don't try to read it all in one go, take a chapter at a time and take breaks in between. Some students find it easier to spot errors if they print out their chapters and read through them, marking any errors in pen, and then correcting them on the computer later.

'Seek and embrace feedback' (Hotaling, 2020) – ask your supervisor to have a look at drafts of your chapters, allowing them plenty of time to do so; sending them your work the night before the submission date is not realistic. Don't expect them to proof read your work for you, but they should certainly give you feedback on the contents and structure of your work.

Submitting your dissertation

Most universities will require you to submit your dissertation online, often through a portal such as Turnitin. Very few universities ask for a hard copy, so you won't be expected to get it printed. You may however want to print out one copy of your dissertation for yourself to keep, as a reminder of all your hard work, and to show to potential employers.

Before submitting, you also need to ensure that there is no inadvertent plagiarism in your dissertation, i.e. using words or ideas that have been published elsewhere without a reference. Most universities will let you upload a draft of your dissertation to their plagiarism software tool such as Turnitin, so you can see if any areas come up highlighted as looking similar to published text – however, do check this, as some universities set up their submission sites so you can only submit your work once.

Marking of the dissertation

Your university will have a set marking criteria for grading your work. If you haven't already been given a copy of this it would be worth asking, as this will explain what you need to do to achieve the boundaries for each grade.

At most universities there are strict marking policies about who marks the dissertation and usually they are marked by at least two lecturers, and usually an external examiner as well. It isn't always possible to do the marking anonymously, as in many cases you will have worked closely with a supervisor who will know your work and even have read drafts, but there should also be a second marker who doesn't know the work so well. The two markers will then discuss the work and agree a mark.

Try not to worry too much at this time. Whilst this is easier said than done, you know how much effort went into your dissertation and with any luck your hard work will be recognised.

Top tip from a student 21.1

I use the read aloud feature on Word when editing, it really helps. Adriana

---

Chapter summary

There are a lot of final pieces to write and put together before you can submit your dissertation, so do ensure you leave plenty of time to design the title page, write the abstract, insert the contents pages, add any lists of figures and tables, as well as organise the appendices. Do check your word counts to ensure the total words are in easy reach of the target you have been set. Proof reading and editing can take time, but they can ensure your dissertation is well written and presented. Make sure you know how and in which format to submit your work, and the time and date by which you must submit, allowing time for any possible delays that could occur. Hopefully you have now completed a major piece of written work of which you are proud.

Check list

- Check the structure of your dissertation, and that the title page, acknowledgements, contents, and appendices are all in the right order
- Check the title page has all the required information
- Ensure your abstract provides a succinct summary of your dissertation including the background, objectives, methods, results and conclusion
- Double check the presentation, layout and word counts
- Leave plenty of time for editing and proof reading as it always takes longer than you think
- Submit!

Further reading

Wilson, A. (2023) *Dissertation Planner*. Peterborough Bookvault Publishing.

22

Preparing for a Viva

Introduction

Whilst at some universities your dissertation thesis may be worth 100% of the mark, at other institutions you may still be required to complete another form of assessment before your final dissertation grade can be awarded. This can include a viva (an oral defence of your thesis), or alternatively an oral or poster presentation of your key findings. This chapter aims to provide guidance on how to get organised for these assessments and ensure you are well prepared on the day.

Viva, short for *Viva Voce* comes from the Latin phrase meaning 'with living voice'. At university the term *viva* is used to mean the oral defence of a dissertation or thesis, and although more common at Master's and PhD level, they can be required on some undergraduate courses too, so do check with your supervisor or programme lead if you are unsure if you need to prepare for one or not.

If you do have to do a viva, then you should try to find out as much as you can about what is expected of you beforehand, including how long the viva will last and who will be conducting it. At undergraduate level the viva may only be for 15 minutes and is likely to be with your supervisor and the second marker.

Preparation is key, so make sure you have recently read your thesis and it is all fresh in your mind. It would be worth doing a quick check of the literature just to make sure you still have a good overview of the literature in your area of study and that there are not any new publications on the same topic as yours.

Try to think about the questions you will likely be asked in the viva. Whilst it would be impossible to think of everything, there are sure to be some questions you could expect. For example, you may be asked:

- To give a brief summary of your research findings
- Why did you choose this topic?
- What reasons did you have for choosing the methodologies that were used, and how did you validate the methods?
- What statistical tests did you do?
- What are the strengths/limitations of your work?
- What are the implications or applications of your findings?
- Was there any risk of bias?
- What would you do differently?
- What research would you do next?

There may even be some unexpected questions that you cannot answer, and that is fine, nobody can know everything and your dissertation cannot cover every topic; perhaps the examiners are just looking to establish the boundaries of all your knowledge. If this is the case it is better to be honest and say you would need to look into that further, than try to waffle and avoid the question.

On the day of your viva, make sure you know the time and venue in advance, and aim to get there at least 15 minutes early. The viva may be relatively informal at undergraduate level, so you don't need to dress up but you may want to dress in a tidy manner. It can be useful to have a copy of your thesis with you, in case there are any particular points that you need to highlight or that need clarification. During the viva, you are entitled to ask for a break at any time, and if the viva is a long one the examiners will suggest a short break at a convenient point, but do feel free to ask the examiners if there is anything you need.

After the viva you will probably be asked to leave the room whilst the examiners deliberate, and then usually very soon afterwards you should get confirmation of your marks.

The viva will mostly be like a very pleasant chat about your work, but if you are nervous, practise breathing exercises to help you remain calm, and of course you can always reach out to somebody at the university, either your supervisor or one of the health and wellbeing advisors, for support.

Instead of a viva, some universities ask students to present the findings of their dissertation as an oral or a poster presentation, or even a Pecha Kucha presentation, and some guidance for these are given below.

Oral presentations

As always find out as much information as you can about the presentation beforehand. In particular find out how long you have to speak and if this includes time for questions or if questions will be in addition.

You will probably be expected to produce some slides to accompany your talk and PowerPoint, Prezi and Canva are popular applications for making slides. The number of slides you need will be determined by the length of your talk, but a very rough guide is no more than one slide per minute (unless you are doing a Pecha Kucha, more on that below).

Slides should be eye catching and possible to read from a distance, so do ensure there is not too much small text on each slide. Choose a coordinating colour scheme and make sure the colour of the text complements the background and can be read easily. For example, if the slides have a white background, black or dark blue are easy to read, whereas a yellow font would be difficult.

It is good to use references on your slides as you would do in any written work, and you can have a slide at the end of your presentation where you list all the references cited.

Bullet points and SmartArt can make your slides look clear and interesting, as opposed to long passages of text which are impossible to read. Graphs, photos, figures, all add interest to your slides and can be a good way of explaining complex information, so do use these where you can. Figure 22.1 shows examples of two PowerPoint slides conveying the results of a dissertation study. Both have the same information but one is more eye catching (even here in greyscale). You don't need to add every detail of your study to your slides, as you can add many of the additional details verbally.

In addition to your slides (or even instead of) you can also use other visual aids. Artefacts, handouts, short videos, samples, or use of a flip chart can all help enhance your talk and keep the audience engaged.

It is a good idea to practise your presentation and time it. You could even film your practice so you can see your performance; you might not realise you are fidgeting or repeatedly using certain words such as 'ummm' until you have seen it for yourself.

It is fine to have notes, as long as you don't read them without looking up at your audience. Some people use the slides as prompts and don't require notes at all, but most students like to have their notes close to hand; even if they don't so much as glance at them, they know they are there if they need them.

On the day of the presentation, make sure you know where the room is and arrive early, so as to upload your slides before the start of the talks.

a)

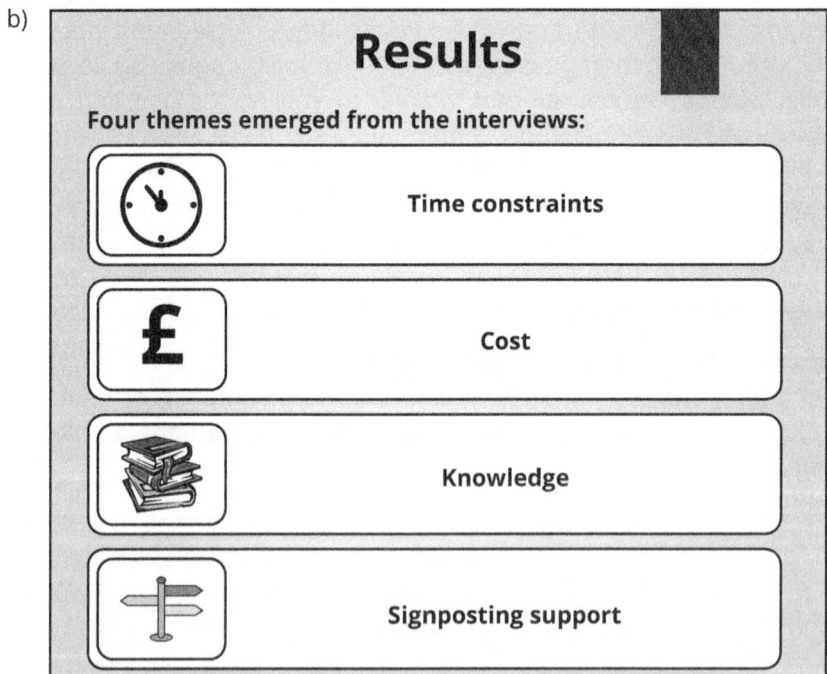

b)

Figure 22.1 Example of slides for an oral presentation

Even though you are likely to know everyone in the audience, you should still introduce yourself and the title of your dissertation. Make sure you talk to the audience, looking at them when you are speaking, rather than down at your notes, but also make sure you pitch the talk at the right level for the people in the room. This is likely to be your supervisor and other lecturers and students, so you can pitch your talk appropriately for an academic audience.

Speak loudly and clearly, and at a pace that will be easy for the audience to follow what you are saying, this may be a bit slower than your usual patter.

If the room has a podium, it would make sense to stand behind that to give your talk, but you might be in classroom, in which case do make sure you don't do too much movement and no pacing up and down.

At the end of your talk, you should finish with a strong closing statement, so the audience knows your talk has finished, and then invite the audience to ask questions: 'Thank you for attention and I would be pleased to answer any questions!'

Pecha Kucha

Pecha Kucha is Japanese for chit chat, and these are oral presentations where the presenter shows 20 slides, and each slide is displayed for 20 seconds before automatically progressing to the next one. This is to encourage a precise presentation with an emphasis on visual images with minimal text. The same advice for oral presentations will apply here also, but in addition you will need to consider the precise timing involved with this sort of presentation.

Poster presentations

If you are required to create a poster as part of your dissertation module, it will be an academic poster, rather than the sort of poster you might design for an advertising or awareness campaign. An academic poster can be used to convey the findings of your research in a visual way using text, tables, graphs, etc., but will contain much more detail than other types of posters.

Check the instructions you have been given in order to prepare your poster. In particular find out if your poster will be printed on paper or if it will be electronic, as many posters are now displayed digitally. If the poster is to be on paper, check the dimensions that your poster needs to be, as posters are often A0 or A1 and may require a specialist printer who can produce a poster of that size. You may also be given particular instructions as to what the minimum font size should be, and if the poster will be displayed in landscape or portrait orientation. PowerPoint is popular for creating posters, but other applications such as Canva and BioRender can be used if preferred.

An example of a template for an academic poster is presented in Figure 22.2. This is only a guide and can be adapted to suit the work you are presenting, and the tables and figures you want to include. In the example in Figure 22.2, the information is organised into columns, so it is clear in which order the poster should be read. If you are using alternative designs make sure the reader knows what to read first and guide them through the information, even using arrows if needed.

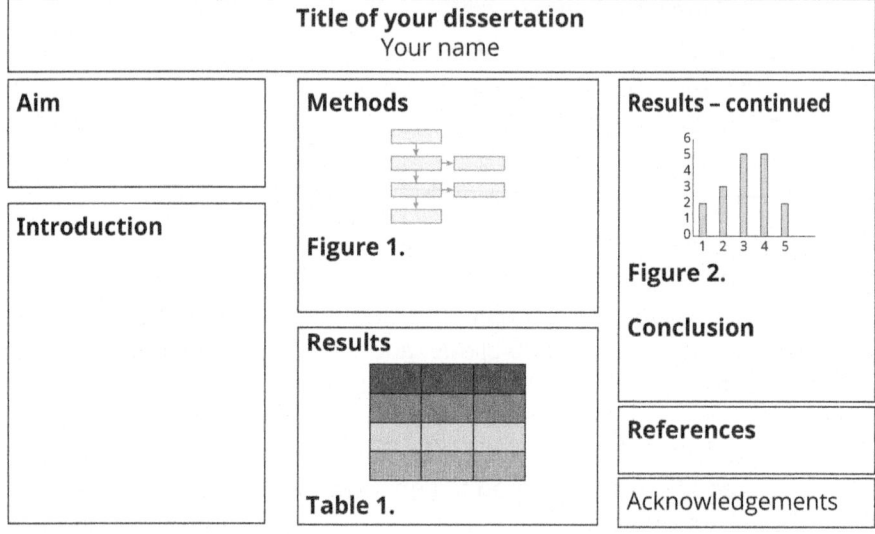

Figure 22.2 Template for an academic poster in landscape orientation

The poster should be visually appealing and make good use of images, figures, graphs, and tables to portray the information rather than being text heavy; if you do need text perhaps it could be presented in the form of bullet points in order to keep the information concise.

Text should be clear to read, so a good size font and double line spacing will help. Choose a font colour that is easy to read, and an overall colour scheme that is attractive; two or three complementary colours are enough to be eye catching without going overboard. Ensure the tables and graphs all complement the colour scheme you have chosen, too.

Don't forget to proof read your poster carefully, as a mistake that looks small on your computer screen can really stand out when printed full size, and it is impossible to correct mistakes once the poster is printed.

On the day of the poster presentation, you may be required to stand next to your poster in order to answer questions about your work. Sometimes you may even be required to give a talk highlighting the key findings that are presented on the poster. This is usually only a short talk, often only five minutes plus questions. You probably won't be able to use slides for this sort of talk, although you would be welcome to have notes, but try to use your poster as a visual aid and point out the key features presented on your poster.

Whether you are required to attend a viva, give an oral presentation, or create a poster in order to defend your thesis, present with confidence and composure. You devised, planned, collected the data and analysed the findings, so nobody knows your dissertation better than you do. It has taken a lot of work to get to this point, so be proud of all you have achieved to reach your goal.

Top tip from a student 22.1

I had confidence going into my viva because I knew I had written every word of that thesis myself and nobody knew the information in it better than me. Kay

---

Chapter summary

At some universities you may be required to defend your thesis in a viva or via a presentation. Prepare for your viva by re-reading your dissertation and try to predict which questions could arise in order to prepare effectively.

If you are giving an oral presentation or a Pecha Kucha, take time to create slides that are informative and well presented, and make sure you practise the timing of your presentation. Speak clearly and with your audience in mind.

If you are doing a poster presentation, make sure you know the format of the poster, and aim to create an eye-catching design that incorporates images and graphs to convey your findings in a visually appealing way. Be prepared to talk about your poster and answer questions.

Whether you are doing a viva, an oral presentation or a poster, present with confidence, as nobody knows your dissertation better than you do.

Check list

- Find out the requirements for the dissertation at your university, including if you need to prepare for a viva or a presentation
- If you are preparing for a viva, re-read your dissertation and think about what questions you could be asked

- If you are doing an oral presentation take your time creating eye catching slides and practise your talk
- If you are doing a poster presentation find out if it needs to be printed or shown electronically

Further reading

Chivers, B. and Shoolbred, M. (2007) *A Student's Guide to Presentations*. London: Sage.

Summary of Part 3

Part 3 of this book, was all about the dissertation, from the planning and deciding on a research question, right up to your final conclusions. At times this may have been challenging but hopefully it gave you the opportunity to apply all the skills you have learnt through out your degree and a chance to showcase your best work.

The last 3 or 4 years of your degree have probably flown by, and you may now be eager to get out into the world of work. You may even feel like you want to know more and may be interested in doing masters degree, or perhaps you enjoyed doing the research for your dissertation you want to do a PhD now or in the future.

When applying for work, or further study, consider all the skills you have gained during your degree, and whilst completing your dissertation such as planning your time and setting targets, critical analysis, presentation etc. and be sure to highlight these on your CV, since these are very much valued by course leaders and future employers.

Finally, good luck with all your future endeavours.

Glossary

Academic argument – where you present a particular view on a topic and debate the evidence for and against the point you are trying to make. Academic arguments need to be convincing and clear but also based on evidence to back up your argument or claim.

Academic integrity – being honest, trustworthy and fair in all your work at university, e.g. avoiding plagiarism and not using AI, etc.

Acknowledgements – at the start of your dissertation you would normally have a page of acknowledgements, where you thank all the people that have helped you get to where you are now.

Acronym – an abbreviation made from the initial letters of words in a phrase.

Active learning – is a way of engaging with information and can include any variety of activities such as problem solving, summarising information, and doing quizzes, to interact with the materials and gain deeper understanding.

Addendum – this usually means an additional item that is added to the end of a report or a document. Lai et al. (2023) describe the 'easy addendum effect', whereby easy tasks are added after completing more difficult tasks, to give the perception that the total work is easier, which can result in greater satisfaction and more work completed.

AI – artificial intelligence is essentially computers that have the ability to process big data and to think like humans.

Alternative hypothesis – can be abbreviated to *HA* and is the opposite of the null hypothesis, it is a statement to say that there is an effect or a statistically significant relationship.

Annotated bibliography – a list of journal papers or books and, under each item, a brief summary and critique of the work.

Anthology – a collection of poems or literary work such as essays or short pieces.

Appendices – at the end of a dissertation, where you put any additional information or raw data. Note appendices is plural whereas appendix is singular.

Argument – in academic writing, the argument is the writer's opinion or stance on a particular topic.

Bias – this could be prejudice or distortion of facts and/or data.

Bibliography – a list of all the sources including further reading that you used to write an essay or report, even those that you did not reference in the text.

Blog – a blog is an online piece of writing like a magazine article.

Blurting – a revision technique where you write down everything you know about a particular topic in a set period of time, then you mark what you have written, correct any mistakes and add anything that may have been left out.

Brain dump – slang for getting lots of information down on paper to stimulate creative thinking.

Canva – an online tool used for creating graphic designs and content.

Case study report – this is usually structured like a laboratory report but the data will be based on a single person (theoretical or real).

Chatbot – a computer software tool that can interact with users and simulate conversations.

ChatGPT – a type of AI chatbot that uses natural language processing so that it is generative, so if given questions and prompts, it can provide human-like answers.

Chicago – a referencing style, named after a city in America, that uses a superscript number in the text and where the reference is added as a footnote.

Chunking – is the breaking down of a large task into a more manageable chunks.

Citing – when you mention or refer to a source. Can also be described as referencing.

Conclusion – the last part of an essay, report or dissertation that summarises and synthesises your findings.

Contents – a list of everything in a book or report.

Continuing professional development (CPD) – learning activities and courses that professionals do to update their knowledge and broaden their experience.

Control group – in experimental protocols, the control group are the participants or samples who do not receive treatment, and to which the experimental group can be compared.

Criticality – at university this refers to being able to interpret, analyse and evaluate information and to encourage academic debate.

Critical review – like an essay written on a particular topic, but focuses on the strengths and limitations of the published literature.

Discussion – a discussion can be a conversation or a debate on a particular topic, but it can also be the section in a practical report or the chapter in a dissertation where you reflect on your findings and what they mean, and compare them to other published sources. You may also consider the strengths and limitations of your work here too.

Dissertation – a large project that includes some form of research that is presented and discussed in written form.

Distance learning – a way of studying online rather than attending in-person lectures.

Easy addendum effect – a way of grouping tasks so you do some difficult tasks followed by an easy task to reduce the perceived difficulty of all the tasks.

Essay – a piece of academic writing on a particular subject that draws on the literature and examines different viewpoints whilst considering the evidence in the form of an academic argument.

Ethics form – An official document that requires you to consider the implications of your research, and to ensure researchers and participants are properly protected.

Exam – a test of your knowledge, usually sat in person and without any reference materials or notes and that is invigilated (i.e. supervised). However, some universities now offer online exams and open book exams as alternative assessments for some courses.

Exemplar – an excellent example or a model answer.

Fake news – information that is false or misleading and not backed by evidence.

Feedback – comments and information you can use to understand why you got the mark you did, and how to do better next time.

Feedforward – focuses on what to do in the future rather than the past.

Flash cards – cards that contain small amounts of information, useful for learning and an aid for revision.

Formative assessment – opportunities to practise an assessment that don't count towards your final marks.

Formative feedback – ongoing feedback and feedback that you receive on drafts or formative assessments.

Generative artificial intelligence (GAI) – has the ability to produce new content, and is based on large language modules that, given the right prompts, can create written pieces, computer code and images.

Glossary – an alphabetical list of words with explanations of what they mean.

Google Scholar – a focused way of using Google to search for academic literature.

Grounded theory – the development of theories based on deep analyses of different types of data that have been collected in order to get a richer understanding of complex phenomena.

Harvard – an American university, but also the name of a referencing style where you cite the name and year, often used in science subjects.

Hypothesis – your prediction of what you think your research will find; this can be based on information you already know.

Introduction – the first paragraph of a report or essay, or the first chapter of a dissertation. The introduction sets the scene and introduces the topic.

Imposter syndrome – an uncomfortable feeling that you aren't good enough or the idea that everyone else knows what they are doing and you don't. You might even feel that your accomplishments are due to chance and not your own abilities. Talking to other people can help you overcome this, so don't let it hold you back.

Journal club – a meeting of students to read and discuss journal papers in a friendly format.

Kolb's Experiential Learning Cycle – this is a method to help you learn from experience, and is divided into four parts: 1) Experience, 2) Reflecting, 3) Thinking and 4) Testing.

Lecture – this is the main method of teaching at university, and is essentially a class where a member of staff will give a talk to students, often accompanied by slides.

Literature review – an overview of all the previously published work and current knowledge on a particular topic.

Logical fallacy – an argument that sounds strong and convincing, but when you analyse it, turns out to be false.

Magazine article – a written piece that is grounded in current research but written more for a lay audience rather than an academic audience, and should be on a topic suitable for publication in a magazine.

Methods – the section in a practical report or the chapter in a dissertation that describes in detail how you performed the experiment, what equipment or questionnaires you used or how you collected the data.

Mnemonic – a method for remembering things, such as using other words to remember lists of facts e.g. in biological sciences, Kindly Put Coffee On For Guest Speaker is used to remember the taxonomy classifications: Kingdom, Phylum, Class, Order, Family Genus, Species. Alternatively you can put things you want to remember into a poem or to music e.g. singing the alphabet.

Module – building blocks or the units of your degree.

Monograph – a piece of research on a specialist topic, usually longer than an essay or a journal paper, like a small book.

Null hypothesis – can be abbreviated to $H0$, and is usually the opposite of your hypothesis, that there are no significant differences or that the effect being studied does not exist, i.e. something that can be disproved when tested.

Oral presentation – speaking to an audience, usually accompanied by slides which are engaging and with limited text. A specified time for the talk will be given and may include time for questions.

OSCOLA – this stands for the Oxford University Standard for Citation of Legal Authorities, and it is a referencing style that puts the references in footnotes and may be accompanied by a bibliography; often used in Law.

Patchwork assignment – a collection of different tasks or written paragraphs on specified topics written over several weeks and then put together.

Pecha Kucha – Japanese for chit chat, these are presentations where you present 20 slides and each slide is shown for 20 seconds before automatically progressing to the next one. The method is used to encourage a precise presentation with an emphasis on visual images with minimal text.

Personal tutor – a lecturer who is there to support you during your time at university and offer guidance to help you with your studies. Some universities have alternative titles such as academic guidance tutor.

Phenomenology – a type of qualitative study that focuses on the individual's lived experiences, and how they understand those experiences and phenomenon within the world around them.

Plagiarism – presenting the work or ideas of other people as your own, often unacknowledged and unreferenced.

Pomodoro technique – a technique used to improve productivity, where you work for 25 minutes, then take a five minute break, do this for two hours, then take a longer break. The idea is that by breaking up the time in this way you can stay more focused.

Portfolio – a collection or compilation of materials that can be used to showcase your skills. An assessment portfolio could include several short tests or small pieces of work collated together.

Poster presentation – information is displayed in poster format, this can be on paper but usually this is online using applications such as PowerPoint or Canva. Posters should be informative and visually engaging. Presenters are usually required to stand by their poster to answer any questions.

PowerPoint – a Microsoft application often used to make slides for presentations or posters.

Practical exam – where you are asked to complete a laboratory practical or some form of practical exercise, and then usually you are asked questions about the practical to further assess your ability and understanding.

Practical report – could also be known as a laboratory report. A concise and structured write up of your findings from a laboratory practical.

Precis – a summary of something such as a text that reviews and condenses the main points.

Primary sources – information that is collected directly such as from interviews or surveys.

Procrastination – putting something off to do another time or delaying.

Programme – sometimes called a course or a degree, but essentially the title of the subject you applied to university to study.

Qualitative research – non-numeric data collected from focus groups or from interviews, used to gather in-depth information on experiences or opinions, frequently used in the social sciences.

Quantitative research – data that is numeric, collected using questionnaires or measurements.

Reference list – the list of references at the end of your report or essay.

Reference style – references can be cited and listed using different styles, so always make sure you know which reference style your university prefers before you start writing.

Referencing – where you acknowledge the source of your information.

Reflection – when you think about yourself and your learning experience.

Reflective learner – a way of thinking about and learning from past experiences.

Report – a specific form of writing that requires you to be factual, concise and formal; often used to present the results of research findings, and structured into different sections which makes it easy to find particular bits of information quickly.

Research proposal – a written plan that explains why the research needs to be conducted and how it will be conducted. This usually should include a brief literature review, an indication of the methods to be used, consideration of ethics, health and safety and data analysis.

Secondary sources – data from previous research such as reports, journal papers and websites.

Self-efficacy – belief in your own ability to perform specific tasks and achieve your goals, a concept first put forward by the psychologist Albert Bandura in 1977.

Seminar – seminars are group discussions of a particular topic that link to your lectures; sometimes you might be given a journal paper to read and then discuss.

Semester – similar to an academic term, but it may be longer; most universities run two semesters per year.

SmartArt – this is a Microsoft application that can insert graphics and visual images to help improve presentation.

Social media – digital platforms that allow the sharing of information and ideas e.g., X, Facebook, Instagram, etc.

Spider diagram – a map of how different ideas relate to each other.

Summative assessment – assessments that count towards your final grades.

Summative feedback – feedback on work that will count towards your final grades.

Synonyms – words with similar meanings.

Syntax – the arrangement of words in a phrase or sentence.

Theoretical framework – an overview of concepts, variables and specific theories that define the scope and provide structure for a research project.

Thesis – usually a large research project, sometimes called a dissertation.

Tutorial – meetings with a lecturer or a tutor, can be an individual meeting or in a group. A tutorial could be a general discussion about how you are getting on, or sometimes you might be given something specific to discuss to support your learning.

Vancouver – a style of referencing that uses numbers in the text and presents the references in numerical order.

Video presentation – a presentation whereby students are asked to pre-record (with a camera or a phone) and edit a film to showcase their public communication skills.

Viva Voce – the exact Latin translation means 'with living voice' but it is used in the context of an oral examination, usually of a dissertation or thesis.

VLE – a virtual learning environment is an online platform used for teaching and hosting educational materials.

Wiki – a blog that multiple people can edit e.g. Wikipedia.

Year of study – what level you are at; most undergraduate degrees are divided into three years, so your year of study would be first, second or third.

References

Adrian-Taylor, S.R., Noels, K.A. and Tischler, K. (2007) Conflict between international graduate students and faculty supervisors: Toward effective conflict prevention and management strategies. *Journal of Studies in International Education*, 11: 90–117.

Anderson, C. (2010) Presenting and evaluating qualitative research. *American Journal of Pharmaceutical Education*, 74: 141. https://doi.org/10.5688/aj7408141.

Armstrong, P. (2010) *Bloom's Taxonomy*. Vanderbilt University Centre for Teaching. https:cft.vanderbilt.edu/guides-sub-pages/blooms-taxonomy/.

Bandura, A. (1977) Self-efficacy: Toward a unifying theory of behavioral change. *Psychological Review*, 84: 191–215.

BBC Bitesize (2024) What is Boolean logic? www.bbc.co.uk/bitesize/guides/zqp9kqt/revision/1#:~:text=Boolean%20logic%20close%20Boolean%20logic,equates%20to%20true%20or%20false.

Baxter, P. and Jack, S. (2008) Qualitative case study methodology: Study design and implements for novice. *The Qualitative Report*, 13: 544–559.

Beatty, L. and Cochran, C.A. (2020) *Writing the Annotated Bibliography: A Guide for Students and Researchers*. Abingdon: Routledge.

Boynton, P.M. (1998) People should participate in, not be subjects of research. *British Medical Journal*, 317: 1521. doi:10.1136/bmj.317.7171.1521a.

Bregman, P. (2020) Your to-do list, is in fact, too long. *Harvard Business Review*. https://hbr.org/2020/08/your-to-do-list-is-in-fact-too-long.

Brown, A. (2014) Implementing active learning in an online teacher education course. American *Journal of Distance Education*, 28: 170–182.

Buczkowski, B. (2023a) How do I write an introduction and literature review? In Reeves, S. and Buczkowski, B. *Mastering Your Dissertation*. Heidelberg: Springer.

Buczkowski, B. (2023b) How do I write the discussion chapter? In Reeves, S. and Buczkowski, B. *Mastering Your Dissertation*. Heidelberg: Springer.

Centre for Teaching and Learning at the University of Oxford (2024) Giving effective feedback. https://www.ctl.ox.ac.uk/giving-effective-feedback.

Chan, C.K.Y. and Hu, W. (2023) Students' voices on generative AI: Perceptions, benefits, and challenges in higher education. *International Journal of Educational Technology in Higher Education*, 20: 43. https://educationaltechnologyjournal.springeropen.com/articles/10.1186/s41239-023-00411-8.

Chemers, M.M., Hu. L-t. and Garcia. B.F. (2001) Academic self-efficacy and first year college student performance and adjustment. *Journal of Educational Psychology*, 93: 55.

Christ, F.L. (1997) *Seven Steps to Better Management of your Study Time*. Clearwater, FL: H&H.

Cirillo, F. (2018) *The Pomodoro Technique: The Life-Changing Time-Management System*. London: Virgin Books.

Cooke, A., Smith, D. and Booth, A. (2012) Beyond PICO: The SPIDER tool for qualitative evidence synthesis. *Qualitative Health Research*, 22: 1435–1443. doi:10.1177/1049732312452938.

Cooper, M. (2018) The results section: Some pointers. *Mick Cooper Training and Consultancy*. https://mick-cooper.squarespace.com/new-blog/2018/11/23/writing-up-results-in-the-psychological-therapies-some-pointers.

Cooper, S. and Nelson, M. (2003) Economy line foods from four supermarkets and brand name equivalents: A comparison of their nutrient contents and costs. *Journal of Human Nutrition and Dietetics*, 16: 339–347.

Cottrell, S. (2008) *The Study Skills Handbook*. 3rd edition. London: Palgrave Macmillan.

Cresswell, J.W. and Poth, C.N. (2024) *Qualitative Enquiry and Research Design*. 5th edition. London: Sage.

Darwin, C. (1871) *The Descent of Man*. London: John Murray.

Doran, G.T. (1981) There's a SMART way to write management's goals and objectives. *Journal of Management Review*, 70: 35–36.

Duncan, J. (no date) Reading critically. www.stetson.edu/other/writing-program/media/CRITICAL%20READING.pdf.

Dyall, S. (2024) Personal communication on the use of ChatGPT for assessment. 31 May 2024.

Dyer, S. (2021) 'I have been a collector of costumes': Women, dress histories and the temporalities of Eighteenth-century fashion. *History*, 106: 578–596.

Economic and Social Research Council (2021) Ethics reviews. www.ukri.org/councils/esrc/guidance-for-applicants/research-ethics-guidance/ethics-reviews/ethics-review-application-forms-and-protocols/.

European Food Safety Authority (EFSA) (2010) Scientific opinion on dietary reference values for water. *EFSA Journal*, 18–38.

European Parliament (2020) What is artificial intelligence and how is it used? www.europarl.europa.eu/topics/en/article/20200827STO85804/what-is-artificial-intelligence-and-how-is-it-used.

Felder, R.M. and Soloman, B.A. (2023) Learning styles and strategies. https://engr.ncsu.edu/wp-content/uploads/drive/1WPAfj3j5o5OuJMiHorJ-lv6fON1C8kCN/styles.pdf.

Ferrari, R. (2015) Writing narrative style literature reviews. *Medical Writing*, 24: 230–235.

Galindo, J.H. (2023) Lecture. https://ablconnect.harvard.edu/lecture-research.

Gibbs, G. (1988) *Learning by Doing: A Guide to Teaching and Learning Methods*. London: Further Education Unit.

Gilmartin, B. (1999) A catalogue of critical reading strategies. In Axelrod, R.B. and Cooper, C.R. *Reading Critically, Writing Well: A Reader and Guid*, 5th edition. New York: Bedford/St. Martin's.

Greenland, S., Senn, S.J., Rothman, K.J., Carlin, J.B., Poole, C., Goodman, S.N. and Altman, D.G. (2016) Statistical tests, P values, confidence intervals, and power: A guide to misinterpretations. *European Journal of Epidemiology*, 31: 337–350.

Gunning, C. (2022) Teaching in reception for the first time. https://early-education.org.uk/teaching-in-reception-for-the-first-time/.

Hart, C. (2018) *Doing a Literature Review*. London: Sage.

Harvard Division of Continuing Education (2021) Why you should make a good night's sleep a priority. https://summer.harvard.edu/blog/why-you-should-make-a-good-nights-sleep-a-priority/.

Health & Care Professions Council (2021) What is reflection? www.hcpc-uk.org/standards/meeting-our-standards/reflective-practice/what-is-reflection.

Heik, T. (2022) What is critical reading? A definition for learning. www.teach-thought.com/literacy/what-is-critical-reading-definition/.

Hirshkowitz, M., Whiton, K., Albert, S.M., Alessi, C., Bruni, O., DonCarlos, L. et al. (2015) National Sleep Foundation's sleep time duration recommendations: Methodology and results summary. *Sleep Health*, 1: 40–43.

Holdsworth, J. (2023) What is AI bias? www.ibm.com/topics/ai-bias.

Hotaling, S. (2020) Simple rules for concise scientific writing. *Limnology and Oceanography Letters*. https://doi.org/10.1002/lol2.10165.

Hopkins, D. and Reid, T. (2018) *The Academic Skills Handbook*. London: Sage.

Information Commissioner's Office (2024) A guide to data protection principles. https://ico.org.uk/for-organisations/uk-gdpr-guidance-and-resources/data-protection-principles/a-guide-to-the-data-protection-principles/.

Institute of Education Writing Centre (2024) Resources for academic reading and writing. Available at www.ucl.ac.uk/ioe-writing-centre/critical-reading-and-writing/critical-review.

Jeanes, Y. (2022) Data collection and presentation. In Reeves, S. and Jeanes, Y. *The Study Skills Handbook for Nutritionists and Dietitians*. Maidenhead: Open University Press.

John Hopkins University (2024) Academic support. https://academicsupport.jhu.edu/resources/study-aids/overcoming-test-anxiety/.

Joyner, R.L., Rouse, W.A. and Glatthorn, A.A. (2018) *Writing the Winning Thesis or Dissertation: A Step-by-Step Guide*. Thousand Oaks, California: Corwin Press Inc.

Kolb, D.A. (1984) *Experiential Learning: Experience as the Source of Learning and Development*. Englewood Cliffs, NJ: Prentice Hall.

Kolb, A. and Kolb, D. (2018) Eight important things to know about the experiential learning cycle, *Australian Educational Leader*, 40, 3. https://search.informit.org/doi/10.3316/informit.192540196827567.

Lai, E.Y., Sevilla, J., Isaac, M.S. and Bagchi, R. (2023) The easy addendum effect: When doing more seems less effortful. *Journal of Applied Psychology*. https://doi.org/10.1037/apl0001130.

Levin, P. (2011) *Excellent Dissertations*. Maidenhead: Open University Press.

Luft, J.S., Jeong, S., Idsardi, R. and Gardner, G. (2022) Literature reviews, theoretical frameworks, and conceptual frameworks: An introduction for new biology education researchers. *CBE – Life Sciences Education*, 21: 3. www.lifescied.org/doi/10.1187/cbe.21-05-0134.

Maier, H.R. (2013) What constitutes a good literature review and why does its quality matter? *Environmental Modelling & Software*, 43: 3–4.

Mair, D. (2019) *The Student Guide to Mindfulness*. London: Sage.

Marr, B. (2023) The difference between generative AI and traditional AI: An easy explanation for anyone. *Forbes*. www.forbes.com/sites/bernard-marr/2023/07/24/the-difference-between-generative-ai-and-traditional-ai-an-easy-explanation-for-anyone/.

Meriam Library, California State University-Chico (2010) Evaluating information – applying the CRAAP test. https://library.csuchico.edu/sites/default/files/craap-test.pdf.

Meyer, S. (2024) The story of Twilight and getting published. https://stephenie-meyer.com/the-story-of-twilight-getting-published/.

Mezrich, B. (2004) *Bringing Down the House: How Six Students took Vegas for Millions*. London: Arrow Books.

Neubauer, B.E., Witkop, C.T. and Varpio, L. (2019) How phenomenology can help us learn from the experiences of others. *Perspectives on Medical Education*, 8: 90–97.

Neville, C. (2010) *The Complete Guide to Referencing and Avoiding Plagiarism*. Maidenhead: Open University Press.

NHS (2024) Better health – drink less. www.nhs.uk/better-health/drink-less/.

Osmond, A. (2016) *Academic Writing and Grammar for Students*. London: Sage.

Pears, R. and Shields, G. (2022) *Cite them Right: The Essential Referencing Guide*. London: Bloomsbury Academic.

Peat, J. and the AI Working Group (2024) *University of Roehampton Generative AI: A Guide for Students*. London: University of Roehampton.

Reeves, S. (2008) Qualitative research methodologies: Ethnography. *British Medical Journal*, 337: a1020.

Reeves, S. and Buczkowski, B. (2023) *Mastering Your Dissertation*. Heidelberg: Springer.

Richardson, W.S., Wilson, M.C., Nishikawa, J. and Hayward, R.S. (1995) The well-built clinical question: A key to evidence-based decisions. *American College of Physicians Journal Club*, 123: A12–A13.

Ridley, D. (2012) *The Literature Review: A Step by Step Guide for Students*. London: Sage.

Rolfe, G., Freshwater, D. and Jasper, M. (2001) *Critical Reflection in Nursing and the Helping Professions: A User's Guide*. Basingstoke: Palgrave Macmillan.

Rudestam, K.E. and Norton R.R. (2014) *Surviving your Dissertation: A Comprehensive Guide to Content and Process*. 4th edition. London: Sage.

Sacred Heart University Library (2020) Organizing academic research papers: Theoretical framework. https://library.sacredheart.edu/c.php?g=29803&p=185919.

Sander, L. (2022) Working from home: 7 tips to boost wellbeing and productivity. *The Conversation*. https://theconversation.com/working-from-home-7-tips-to-boost-wellbeing-and-productivity-187427.

Schön, D.A. (1983) *The Reflective Practitioner: How Professionals Think in Action*. New York: Basic Books. (Reprinted in 1995.)

Shean, M. (2019) Don't calm down! Exam stress may not be fun but it can help you get better marks. *The Conversation*. https://theconversation.com/dont-calm-down-exam-stress-may-not-be-fun-but-it-can-help-you-get-better-marks-124517.

Siegel, J. (2024) The art of the prompt: How to get the best out of generative AI. https://news.microsoft.com/source/features/ai/the-art-of-the-prompt-how-to-get-the-best-out-of-generative-ai/.

Subramanyam, R. (2013) Art of reading a journal article: Methodically and effectively. *Journal of Oral and Maxillofacial Pathology*, 17: 65–70.

Taylor, H., Garnham, W.A. and Ormerod, T. (2019) Active essay writing: Encouraging independent research through conversation. In Betts, T., Garnham, W.A. and Oprandi, P. (eds) *Disrupting Traditional Pedagogy: Active Learning in Practice*. University of Sussex Library. https://doi.org/10.20919/9780995786240.

Tress Academic (2019) What sort of journal paper to write? https://tressacademic.com/paper-types/.

UK Chief Medical Officer (2019) Physical activity guidelines. www.gov.uk/government/publications/physical-activity-guidelines-uk-chief-medical-officers-report.

University of Oxford (2024) Use of generative AI tools to support learning. www.ox.ac.uk/students/academic/guidance/skills/ai-study.

University of Southampton Library (2024) Writing your dissertation – guides for success. https://library.soton.ac.uk/writing_the_dissertation/literature_review.

University of Tasmania (2024) Systematic Reviews for Health: 7. *Boolean Operators*. https://utas.libguides.com/SystematicReviews/Boolean.

University of York (2024) Academic writing: A practical guide. https://subject-guides.york.ac.uk/academic-writing/dissertations.

UnJaded Jade (2018) New revision technique that ACTUALLY works: 'Blurting'. *YouTube*. www.youtube.com/watch?v=CgrCo1J9A44.

U.S. Food and Drug Administration (2023) Spilling the beans: How much caffeine is too much? www.fda.gov/consumers/consumer-updates/spilling-beans-how-much-caffeine-too-much.

van der Velden, M. (2021) 'I felt a new connection between my fingers and brain': A thematic analysis of student reflections on the use of pen and paper during lectures. *Teaching in Higher Education*. doi: 10.1080/13562517.2020.1863347.

Van der Weel, F.R., Van der Meer, A.L.H. (2024) Handwriting but not typewriting leads to widespread brain connectivity: A high density EEG study with implications for the classroom. *Frontiers in Psychology*, 14. www.frontiersin.org/journals/psychology/articles/10.3389/fpsyg.2023.1219945/full.

Wallace, M. and Wray, A. (2021) *Critical Reading and Writing for Postgraduate Students*. London: Sage.

World Medical Association (2022) WMA Declaration of Helsinki – Ethics Principals for Medical Research Involving Human Subjects. www.wma.net/policies-post/wma-declaration-of-helsinki-ethical-principles-for-medical-research-involving-human-subjects/.

Zimmerman, B.J. (2000) Self-efficacy: An essential motive to learn. *Contemporary Educational Psychology*, 25: 82–91.

Index

Page numbers in *italics* refer to figures; page numbers in **bold** refer to tables.